Vibrational Reiki™

Level One Manual

Francine Milford

Vibrational Reiki™ Level One Manual by Francine Milford

Copyright © 2019 Francine Milford and its licensors. All rights reserved.

Other Editions 2014, 2013, 2007

Disclaimer

The information given in this book is not meant to diagnose or give recommendations and advice about the treatment of any illness. If you are ill, consult your physician or primary health care practitioner before pursuing any form of therapy on your own. This author makes no claims or guarantees to your healing or self-transformation.

ID: 978-0-615-16844-9

Photography by Francine Milford

Illustrations by Francine Milford

No part of this publication may be reproduced or transmitted in any form or by any means electronic or mechanical, including photocopy, recording, or any information storage and retrieval system, without permission in writing from both the copyright owner and the publisher.

Table of Contents

Chapter One..7

What is Reiki?..7

Chapter Two..9

Reiki Level One training................................9

Chapter Three..11

The Attunement Process........................11

    Gassho....................................12

    Tree Grounding Meditation............12

    Cleansing Process......................13

Chapter Four..15

The Hands in Reiki....................................15

    Beaming................................17

Chapter Five..19

The Chakra System................................... 19

Chapter Six..29

Byosen..29

Chapter Seven...33

Hand Positions for Healing Self................33

Chapter Eight..............................**41**

Hand Positions for Others......................41

    Closing...................................47

DAY TWO

Chapter Nine................................**49**

Introduction to the Tuning Fork....................49

Chapter Ten..................................**53**

The Genesis tuning fork...........................53

    Infinity symbol on chakras.............60

    Infinity symbol (seated)................61

    Infinity symbol partner................63

Chapter Eleven..............................**65**

    Additional symbols.....................65

    Body Scanning........................70

    Aura Scanning........................72

    The Vibrational Reiki™ Session.....72

Client In-Take form.........................**77**

Protocols for Spot Treatment...............**79**

About the Author...........................**83**

Chapter One
What is Reiki?

(The following information has been taken from my Usui Reiki Level One manual)

What is Reiki?

Reiki, (pronounced ray-key), in the Japanese Character system, is a combination of two separate words. "Rei" meaning "universal, spirit, a boundless essence" and "Ki" meaning "life force energy". Together their meaning is roughly "Universal Life Energy", or "Universal life force energy".

Life force energy resides in everything you see around you, yourself included. All animals, plants, humans, have life force energy. The ancient discipline of Qigong is the practice of gathering up this energy and directing it into parts of the body. When a person dies, this life force energy departs the body.

In practice, Reiki is a safe, natural, and holistic way of treating yourselves and others from many acute and chronic conditions. It helps to bring about physical, mental, spiritual, and emotional well-being.

Reiki is not a substitute for traditional medicine. No Reiki practitioner should ever tell a client that they can "cure" an illness or advise their client to stop taking any prescribed medicines or to stop seeing their doctor. This is very bad business, and the Reiki practitioner must stay out of the choices their clients are making. It is both unethical and illegal to make suggestions such as these to any client.

Conditions that Reiki may improve include:

- Stress
- menstrual problems
- pain
- insomnia
- anxiety
- tension
- headaches
- asthma
- anxiety attacks
- intestinal gas
- many, many more…

Exercise #1:

As an exercise to feel this energy, begin by rubbing your hands together for one minute. Be sure to bring your mind's focus to your hands while you are doing this. Now, slowly and gently, pull the palms of your hands apart to about 1" to 3" away from each other. Continue this bringing in and taking apart for a few minutes. Be aware of the energy that you are feeling. That is your life force energy.

Exercise #2:

Find a partner for this exercise. Rub the palms of your hands briskly together again as you did in the previous exercise. Be sure to bring your mind's focus to the palms of your hands. This time, bring your hands to 1" to 3" away from your partner's hands. Slowly bring your hands together, without touching, and take them apart again for a few minutes. Be aware of the energy that you are feeling. Be aware of your partner's energy field.

Exercise 2:

To help you experience the possibilities of working with the energy, I want you to do the following exercise: Rub your hands briskly together again. Bring your mind's focus to your hands.

Take your hands and place them, palms facing each other in front of you. I want you to play with this energy by pulling your hands apart and bringing them together.

You can play with expanding the energy in front you. Make the energy between your hands larger and larger each time you come together and pull apart.

You can also compress this energy into an egg shape of concentrated energy and place this egg of energy into a particular body area, or organ.

It is very helpful in your Reiki practice, to become familiar and learn to work with energy. It is NOT necessary to become an energy expert in order to practice Reiki; it is just one more tool you can place in your little black bag of healing systems.

Write down any sensations or experiences you had while doing this exercise:

_____
_____
_____
_____
_____
_____
_____

The History of Reiki (updated)

About Mikao Usui

Usui was born on August 15, 1865 in the village of Taniai. At the age of four, Mikao Usui entered a Tendai Buddhist school where he studied Kiki (a form of Qigong). Later, Usui traveled to Chine and Europe furthering his studies of medicine and religion.

Usui married Sadako and fathered a son, Fuji, and daughter, Toshiko. He became the Secretary to Shinpin Goto, head of the Department of Health and Welfare. Later, he becomes the Mayor of Tokyo and a member of the Rei Jyutu Ka, a metaphysical group that was dedicated to developing psychic abilities.

In March of 1922, Usui was upset with both a failing business and a failing personal life. He went to Mt. Karama to fast, meditate and repent. He was looking for a solution to his problems.

He enrolled in the 21-day training that was offered at the Tendai Buddhist Temple which was called, Isyu Guo. It was during this training period that Usui received the answers to his problems, Reiki. Usui realized that he had not only received a spiritual awakening, but also the ability to heal. Usui called his system of healing, **"Shin-Shin Kai-Zen Usui Reiki Ryo-Ho."** Translated, it means, "The Usui Reiki Treatment Method for Improvement of Body and Mind." Later this was simplified to **Usui Reiki Ryoho** meaning, "Usui Reiki Healing Method."

In April of 1922 Usui opened the "Usui Reiki Ryoho Gakkai," as a healing society in Tokyo. Translated in English, the name of this society would mean, "Usui Reiki Healing Method." In addition to the creation of the Usui Reiki Ryoho Gakkai, Usui opened a Reiki Clinic in Harajuku, Aoyama, in Tokyo. At the clinic, Usui taught classes and offered treatments. Usui taught his Reiki classes in Three Levels as follows:

- **Shoden (First Degree).** Translated, this means, "First Teachings." This was taught in parts: Loku-Tou, Go-Tu, Yon-Tou, San-Tou
- **Okuden (Second Degree).** Translated, this means, "Inner Teaching." It was taught in two parts: Okuden-Zen-Ki and Okuden-Koe-Ki.
- **Shinpiden (Master Level).** Translated, this means, "Mystery Teaching." It was taught in two parts: Shihan-Ka Ku (assistant teacher) and Shihan (venerable teacher).

It was said that Usui only taught three symbols, the same ones that we have been using in Level Two training. Somehow, others were added to the system later.

When Tokyo suffered a devastating earthquake in 1923, Usui and his students went to the area to help those affected by the disaster. This caused a great interest in Reiki by those who were most touched by it, or who witnessed the great affects that Reiki had on those who were suffering. The interest in receiving and learning Reiki grew so much that Usui ended up building a larger clinic in Nakano, Tokyo.

Usui-Sensei is said to have been friends with the Emperor Meiji who wrote down many verses in a large book. Among his writings was five admonitions that Usui later had his students chant in the morning and evening while in Gassho. These admonitions were as follows:

1. **Don't get angry today**
2. **Don't be grievous**
3. **Express your thanks**
4. **Be diligent in your business**
5. **Be kind to others**

You will find variations of these admonitions in many writings and teachings. But the underlying theme and intent will remain the same.

Mikao Usui began being called Usui-Sensei by his students. Usui's pen name is Gyohan. The word 'Sensei' means 'teacher.' It is a word of earned honor.

Usui-Sensi began to travel so that he could teach and treat more people.

Before his death at age 62 on March 9, 1926, Usui-Sensi had taught more than 2,000 people the gift of Reiki. After his death, Usui-Sensei students created a memorial stone next to his gravestone at the Saihoji Temple in Suginami, Tokyo.

Usui-Sensei had trained 22 teachers before his passing. At the society, the title of president has passed from Usui-Sensei to the following:

Mr. J. Ushida

Mr. Yoshiharu Watanabe

Mr. Toyoichi Wanami

Ms. Kimiko Koyama

Mr. Kondo

About Chujiro Hayashi

A student of Usui-Sensei, Hayashi was a medical doctor in the Navy. After receiving his Reiki Master training, Hayashi opened his own Reiki Clinic and school called **Hayashi Reiki Kenkyukai**. Hayashi-Sensei recorded his treatment plans and kept a diary of what hand positions worked best for certain conditions. He recorded his findings in the **Reiki Ryoko Shinshin**, which translated means, *Guidelines for Reiki Healing Method*.

Up until this time, Usui had his clients sit in a chair to receive their Reiki session. Hayashi-Sensei had his clients lay on the table instead. He also used several Reiki practitioners at one time to treat the client. Prior to World War Two, Japan was gearing up for their attack on the United States and called in Hayashi to give them some strategic war information. Hayashi refused and was called a traitor. Since he no longer wanted to take part in a war but wanted to save face for himself and his family, he performed the traditional ritual suicide called *Seppuku* on May 11, 1940.

Hawayo Takata

Hawayo Takata was born of Japanese immigrants on Dec. 24, 1900 on the Island of Kauai, Hawaii. Widowed at an early age, Takata worked hard to support herself and her children. When she was diagnosed with a tumor, instead of choosing surgery, Takata went to Hayashi's clinic for help. Once there, Takata received treatments from two practitioners every day. In four months, Takata was healed and began to receive her level one training into Reiki.

After working for Hayashi-Sensei for a year, Takata earned her level two degree. In February of 1938, Takata became a Reiki Master. She established a clinic in Hilo on the Big Island and began to teach and give treatments.

Up until 1970, Takata did not give out the Master initiation to her students. But after this time, she decided to offer the initiation into Reiki mastership along with a hefty price tag- $10,000.

She died on December 11, 1980 leaving behind 22 Reiki Masters. Her granddaughter Phyllis Fuoromoto took on the title of Grandmaster and created the Reiki Alliance, which is still operating today.

There is still discussion about the correct lineage of Reiki, and there are those that claim that the title of Grandmaster was never passed to her. Some believe that Reiki never left Japan and that the Reiki information that left Japan has changed and become 'Westernized." This is true in many respects. While some things have been added, other items have been deleted.

The Symbol for Reiki

The Ancient Form

Pictured below is the ancient form of the symbol, Reiki. This is called the Kanji style. It is from the ancient Japanese language. There still exist today many dialects in Japan. Each dialect has its own symbols and meaning. Some are the same (universal) while others are quite close to their own region. In the Japanese language, there is no "R" sound. When Dr. Usui started to use Reiki in Japan, he did not call it Reiki. In fact, he did not call it anything. It wasn't until his death that his remaining students came together to form the "Reiki system of natural healing". In Japan, Reiki is not pronounced (ray-key). Instead, it is called, (lay-key). The "R" sound in Japan is actually an "l" sound.

In this ancient form of symbol, there is a lot more information that is given. Each line and stroke is a meaning unto itself. Putting together the lines and strokes make up the story, the information that is the symbol. Much meaning has been lost to the present day world of the total meaning of this Kanji symbol since its dialect is no longer practiced in Japan.

In the modern form of the Reiki symbol, we clearly see two separate and unique symbols together. The top symbol is "Rei" and the bottom symbol should be more familiar to us as "Ki". The Rei symbol has many definitions and meanings. Among them are the following information connected to the Reiki symbol: Universal, Spirit, Ghost, Supernatural, and Consciousness of spirit.

The Ki symbol is called many things around the world. In China this Ki is called Chi, or Qi. In Sanskrit and India, this Ki is called Prana. In the Native American language, Ki would be called the Great Spirit. Whatever it is called, Ki means life force energy. Ki is the energy of life that surrounds every living thing. The Chinese uses this knowledge of life force energy in their practice of acupuncture. It is our contention here that Reiki affects the energy of the person you are working on. When a client's Ki, or energy life force, is low, they are more prone to illnesses. Giving a client Reiki can help enhance their immune system and restore their weakened "Ki".

Ancient symbol   Modern symbol

Chapter Two

The Reiki Healing Session

About using Reiki

Do not force or push the energy, keep your own ego and energy out of it.

- Do not believe that nothing is happening. Something is ALWAYS happening.
- Become detached from the results. Reiki will do what it needs to do.
- Turn over the results to God (or whichever other name Source comes by for you).
- Remember, you cannot make any mistakes with Reiki, you are doing just fine!
- Use your intuition and follow your impressions no matter how weird they may seem.
- Be aware that people need to ask for Reiki healing for it to work in their lives.
- People have free will and they may choose (for whatever reason) NOT to be healed.
- Do not judge your own perception of the flow of energy from your hands.
- Sometimes what you feel is NOT what the client feels. Keep ego out of it.

Can I give or get a bad treatment?

The answer is YES! You can give a bad treatment if your energies are scattered. If I am feeling off balance, I will cancel my scheduled appointments before I send them any of that kind of energy. It isn't fair to them and it isn't fair to you to continue with your planned appointments if you know in your heart that you are not up to it. Money isn't everything!

There are very, very, precious few Reiki practitioners (or energy workers in general), that I, myself, would go to for a treatment. I am very sensitive to people's energy fields and the slightest problems that the practitioners may be dealing with could easily throw my own balance off. Remember, when you are receiving a treatment, you are letting your guard (protection) down and allowing the practitioner to work within your energy fields.

What if my client doesn't feel anything?

There will come times where the energy does not seem to flow through into the client. There may be no apparent reason for this to happen. Even though you feel that you did all the right preparations, hand positions, etc. you may feel that you did not get the required results. So what happened? Remember that the client does have the free will to accept or reject the Reiki energy. Even if they come to you and say, "Please do something for me" subconsciously they may be holding on to their illness for whatever reason. It could be a lesson that they need to learn. Until they learn that lesson, they need their dis-ease. It is a teacher for them. Do not take that away from them.

How to perform a typical Reiki session

The client will lie on a massage table fully clothed. I usually ask that the client remove their shoes and watch (jewelry optional). A normal Reiki healing session lasts about one hour. The first half of the session is performed with the client lying face up, and the second half is performed with the client face down.

The client may choose to sit in a chair. All ways are acceptable. You may have a sheet available in case the client feels chilled or you may begin the session by covering them with the sheet from the start.

But before the client even arrives for their session, I begin a small cleansing and purification ritual for my room. If you are a Reiki II, III, or Master practitioner, you begin by drawing the symbols you will be using in the healing session on each wall, the ceiling, the floor, and on the table itself. (If you want, you can also draw these symbols on the back of your massage table).

For those of you who are Reiki I Practitioner, you will then just stand in front of each wall, ceiling, floor, and table and "beam" or "send" Reiki energy for at least 5 minutes. After I am finished with the room, I then draw the symbols on each of my Chakras, including the Chakras in the palms of my hand.

I sit in Gassho meditation (which we will discuss later on in the course) to help me focus my intention for the healing session. At this point, any meditation will help you to focus your intention. Breathe slowly and deeply to relax your mind and body.

What does a Reiki session feel like?

Many people, many experiences. Some people feel Reiki as warmth. Others feel hot energy, cold hands, clammy hands, or even nothing at all. The sensations may even change throughout the course of the treatment. All is acceptable. If they feel nothing at all, it does not mean that they did not receive Reiki. Some people are more sensitive to the energies that are around them, others are not. Every time you set out to give a Reiki treatment, know that you are passing this healing energy onto the client. What the client chooses to do with this energy is up to them, not you.

When we can keep our human ego out of the healing session, the entire session will run more smoothly. Without our ego there are no "Should" or ."Shouldn't", no "right" way or "wrong" way. If we remember that each one of us is unique and that each healing session will also be unique, then we can also accept the fact the "we" are not healing anyone. We are merely facilitators to the energy that is called Reiki. And since I believe that Reiki energy will go where it is most needed in the body, then I am also not responsible for the outcomes of a Reiki treatment.

Of course, good and positive feedback is always nice to hear after a Reiki treatment, but in the final analysis, the healing season will be what it is meant to be no matter how we think we can control the outcome.

The Law of Attraction in Reiki:

When someone comes to you, they need you (or they have a lesson for you to learn)

Chapter Three

The Attunement Process

What is an Attunement?

An attunement is given to every Reiki student by the Reiki master. The attunement is a process of opening the student's energy centers to connect to and accept the flow of Reiki energy into their body. Student will sit in a chair with their feet on the floor and their hands in Gassho position. The Reiki teacher will play either a guided meditation or just some soft music. The lights will be lowered. I always explain to the students what I will be doing BEFORE I begin the attunement process. This way, it puts them at ease and they can just relax throughout the process.

Following training, each student is expected to go home and practice the hand positions for healing themselves that they were taught every night for at least 21 nights (longer if they feel more is needed). Students should pick a particular time, day or night, where they will be able to do the Reiki hand positions on themselves undisturbed for one hour. This is called the *Cleansing Process* and is very important for the Reiki practitioner. Students should NOT continue on to Reiki Level Two training until they have completed the Cleansing Process.

How to Prepare for the Attunement

To prepare physically, the student should eat a very light meal or no meal at all one hour before the attunement time. The student should also perform some type of cleansing and purification ritual before the attunement. A few ideas for those of you who are new to cleansing and purifications rituals would be some of the following:

- Take a shower and imagine your entire body and aura being cleansed of impurities.
- Smudging
- Meditation

*Smudging.** Smudging is the burning of white sage. To perform this ceremony you will need to purchase a twig of white sage and a container to hold the ashes in. Light the sage and then blow the fire out. What you will have left is smoke. It is this smoke that you will use for the smudging process. You will take this smoke and swirl it all around you. Native Americans use smudging as a way of cleansing and purification. You can also take this smoke to the corners of the room that you are going to be sitting in to receive your attunement.

*Meditation.** You should sit quietly before the appointed attunement time to calm and center yourself. Free your mind of all the days' obligations and relax. There are some excellent meditation tapes on the market if you need to practice before the attunement.

Gassho

What is Gassho?

Gassho is a form of meditation that Dr. Usui taught to his students. This is a focused meditation and requires much practice and patience. Start with only a few minutes at a time and build up to the 20 minutes.

To Do: Close your eyes. Take a slow and deep breath through your nose. Release the breath slowly through your mouth. Repeat breathing in and out. Feel your body begin to relax. Feel your mind begin to relax. Fold your hands together (as if in prayer) in front of you. Focus your attention at the point where your two middle fingers meet. Try to forget everything else. If you begin to think of other things, observe the thought and then let it go. Breathe in and Relax. Exhale out and Let Go.

Assignment: Every day for 21 days practice the Gassho meditation. Spend 5-30 minutes a day in this meditation.

Tree Grounding Meditation

Before you begin any energy work, you must first use a grounding technique to protect and balance you throughout the session. One such grounding technique that I have used is called the Tree Grounding Meditation. The Tree Grounding Meditation was a technique I learned when I had begun my Qigong practice, and now I use it whenever I need to ground myself. To begin this technique, you will need to stand with your feet at least 6" apart.

I begin my envisioning myself standing tall, like a tree, with my feet flat on the ground. I feel my body as that of a tree, solid and strong. I feel the limbs of my body as solid and strong branches of a tree. See and feel that tree very, very vividly.

I see roots coming out of the bottom of my feet—they dig deep into the ground beneath my feet, deeper, deeper, and deeper. They tunnel their way to the center of the earth. The deeper they dig into the earth, the stronger my tree becomes.

The roots go down to the center of the Earth where there is a round, red core. The roots begin to wrap themselves around the core of the earth. I feel very secure, and there is a solid feeling in my feet and legs.(I then take the opportunity to draw up the energy of the Earth into my body for an energizing effect.)

To Perform this Meditation:

Close your eyes. Inhale, and pull the energy up the roots of your right foot, into your right foot, up your right leg, and into your lower abdominal area.

Feel the energy accumulate within your lower abdominal region.

Exhale, and push this energy down your left leg, out your left foot, and back down the roots to the center of the earth.

Continue inhaling and pulling the energy up into the right side of the body and exhaling out down the left side of your body back in the earth. Form this energy loop, this connection and feel it grow stronger and stronger.

When you are ready, release your connection to the earth, thank the earth and open your eyes.

What is the Cleansing Process?

After receiving your first Reiki attunement, changes begin to happen in the body. You must first heal yourself before you heal others. By giving yourself daily doses of Reiki energy, you will begin to notice subtle changes taking place. Depending on where you are currently on your spiritual path will determine what type of changes you will notice. For me, I slept better, felt calmer and more at peace. But some experience a clearing.

If you are angry, upset, frustrated, and have chaos all around you, then the energy you will be sending to your client may have some of these energies mixed in with it. Heal your life and your emotions FIRST before you begin to help others. Don't be afraid to practice Reiki on yourself for fear of what emotions or experiences you will bring to the surface. Know this: you will NEVER be given more that the Universe knows you can handle.

While giving yourself Reiki treatments for the next 21 days, you may find it helpful to jot down a few of your experiences during this Cleansing Process. Journaling is a healthy and healing activity. When writing about your experiences, include any sounds you hear and odors you smell. Include all of your senses in the viewing of your experiences.

Don't become discouraged if you don't see anything or feel anything. Time and practice will help you to develop these extra senses of yours so that one day you will be able to. And if this takes longer than 21 days, that is alright too. Don't rush the process.

Week One

    Day 1

    Day 2

    Day 3

    Day 4

    Day 5

    Day 6

    Day 7

Week Two

    Day 1

    Day 2

    Day 3

    Day 4

    Day 5

    Day 6

    Day 7

Week Three

    Day 1

    Day2

    Day 3

    Day 4

    Day 5

    Day 6

    Day 7

Chapter Four

The Hands in Reiki

How to Hold your Hands

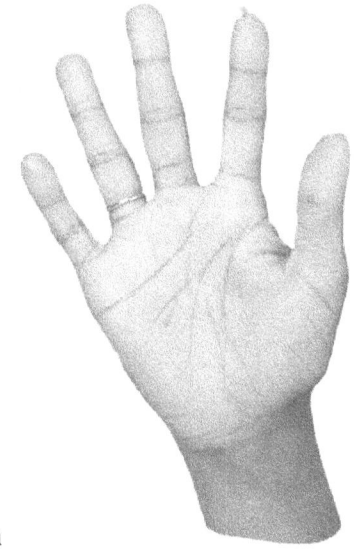

#1 - Open

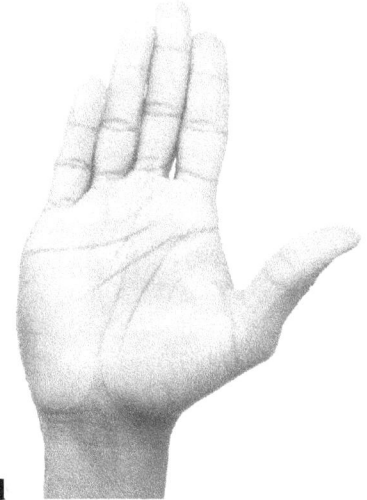

#2 – Closed

A common lesson taught to students is that when performing your hand positions, you should strive to keep your fingers together (#1). Not only are students encouraged to keep their fingers together, they are also encouraged to keep their hands cupped. It is believed that you can better focus and gather energy when your fingers are closed together and your hands are slightly cupped. Some lineages require their students to keep their hands perfectly flat, not cupped. As far as what I teach, I encourage my students to do what feels right for them. If you feel comfortable in a certain hand position, then use that hand position.

In the picture (#2) the fingers are apart. This is said to disperse energy. This is another technique that we will discuss in other Reiki levels of training - the dispersing of energy. For now, try to practice your hand positions with your fingers closed. Concentrate on the energy that is coming from your hands and set your intention before, during and after each Reiki session. Those types of exercises are used in Yoga classes for releasing tensions in the body.

Hand Positions - How do I hold my Hands?

There are many ways in which you may choose to hold your hands in the Reiki healing session. The old way insisted that both of your hands must be touching each other in each and every hand position. If you wanted to work on both hip positions simultaneously, this would be impossible if you followed this logical pattern. What you would have to do is to use both hands on the left hip, then use both hands on the right hip.

My own belief in this matter is that it isn't important for both hands to ALWAYS be touching each other in the hand positions. The MOST important thing I believe is that your focus and intention be squarely on your client. I would like to talk about some of the ways you can place your hands in a healing session.

Which Hand Position is best for me?

As for which is best to use? This is what I would recommend. I would use Position #1 for Hips, and specific "trouble" spots that the client is having. I would use Position #2 for head, face, and front and back Chakra areas. I would use Position #3 for hand positions for the front and back of the client's body, including the knees and ankles. Then, finally, I would Position #4 for hand positions of the head, face, elbows, wrists, hands, hips, knees, and ankles.

The Major Hand Positioning

There are four major hand positions that are used in a typical Reiki session. They are:

- **Hands Crossed**
- **Hands Side by Side**
- **Hand over Hand**
- **Hand Sandwiching**

Position #1-Hands Crossed

In this position, one hand is placed over the area you want to send extra Reiki healing energy into, and the other hand is placed over top the first hand in a crisscross pattern. It doesn't matter which hand goes down first.

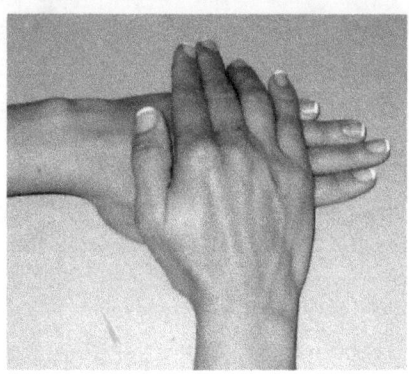

Position #2-Side by Side

In this hand position both hands are placed together with the sides of the two hands touching each other. Fingers are pointed in the same direction. Practitioners who use this hand position usually do their hand positions down one side of the client's body and repeat them on the other side of the client's body.

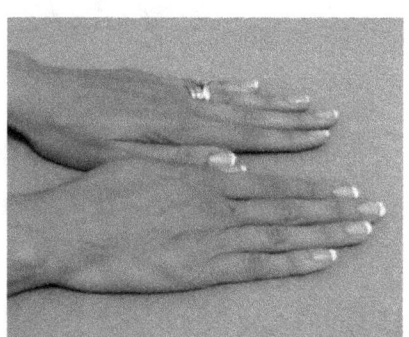

Position #3 - Hand over Hand

This hand position is taught to Reiki students and is what I use in my own Reiki sessions. In this hand positioning, one hand is placed on the area which is to receive Reiki first, the second hand is then placed on a direct line of the first hand. The fingertips of the first hand are covered with the bottom of the palm of the second hand.

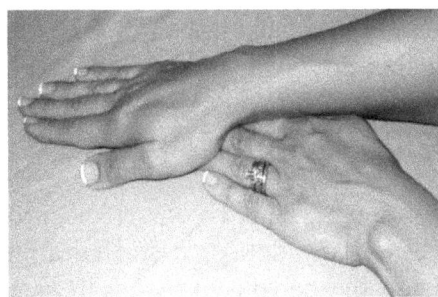

Position #4 - Sandwiching

This hand position requires one hand on top of a particular body area as the other hand is under that particular area of the body. This is a great hand position for the joints, hands and feet. Use this hand position for the elbows, wrists, hands, hips, knees, ankles, and the feet. It doesn't matter what hand is on top or what hand is underneath.

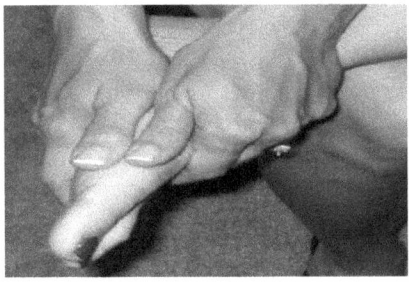

Beaming

What is Beaming?

Beaming is a technique to teach students how they can "send" Reiki energy to someone across the room, across the state, and across the world.

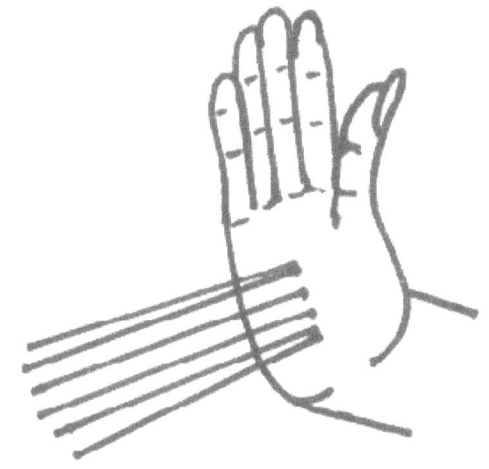

There are many ways a student can do this and I have listed some of my favorite techniques:

- Stand in front of the person, or thing, you want to send Reiki energy to. Breathe in Reiki energy and send the energy through your hands to the object you want to send Reiki energy to. Aim the palm of your hands right at it. I like to think of the person being in a big cocoon and I am filling the cocoon with Reiki energy.
- You can use a photograph and "beam" Reiki energy into the photograph

- You can use a proxy, such as a baby doll, and send Reiki energy to the baby doll and intend to go to a specific person.
- Write the person's name/information on a piece of paper and "beam" Reiki energy right into the piece of paper.

A typical beaming or long distant healing takes usually 5 to 15 minutes. It very rarely takes longer than that. I have heard of people giving a proxy a one hour treatment and "beaming" that treatment to someone far away. When beaming, some Reiki practitioners imagine the Reiki energy flowing out of their hands like rays from the sun. It is this ray of energy that can be directed to a particular area of the body, a plant, or a pet. Below is a picture of how a Reiki practitioner can send Reiki energy into their own feet.

Assignment 1: Sit in a comfortable position where you can still see your feet. Now, inhale the Reiki energy and send it to your feet using the Beaming Technique. Follow photograph #1. Send this energy for 5-15 minutes.

Assignment 2: Find a photograph of someone you would like to send Reiki energy to, or write on a piece of paper the information about someone you would like to send Reiki energy to. Hold this piece of paper between your hands. Take a deep breath of Reiki energy and send this energy to the paper, or photograph, between your hands. Continue to send this energy for 5-15 minutes.

Assignment 3: Find yourself a "proxy". This can be a baby doll or a stuffed animal. Now, envision the person you want to send Reiki to and see that person as the proxy. Begin the Reiki hand positions as you would if the person was there in front of you. Think of the person as you send Reiki energy into the proxy. You can do either a quick treatment lasting only 5-15 minutes treatment, or a full body treatment lasting up to one hour. It is up to you.

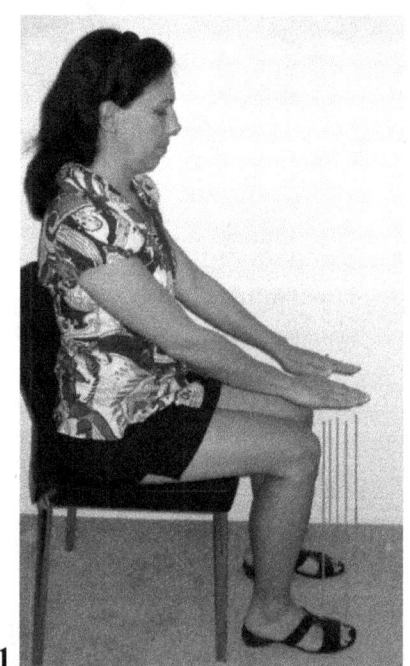
#1

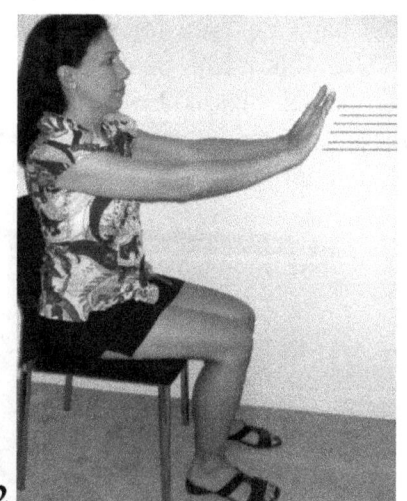
#2

Assignment 4: Following photograph #2 send Reiki energy to every wall, ceiling and floor in every room of your home. Send Reiki to every object in that room. Spend 1-5 minutes on each object. When finished, you might want to go outside and Reiki your plants, car, etc.

Additional ways to use Technique

You can even beam Reiki energy to your home, your car, and to your plants. You can beam Reiki energy to a photograph of someone you love. Just hold the photograph between your hands and send them Reiki energy.

Chapter Five

The Chakra System

The Seven Major Chakras (Front)

The Seven Major Chakras (Front)

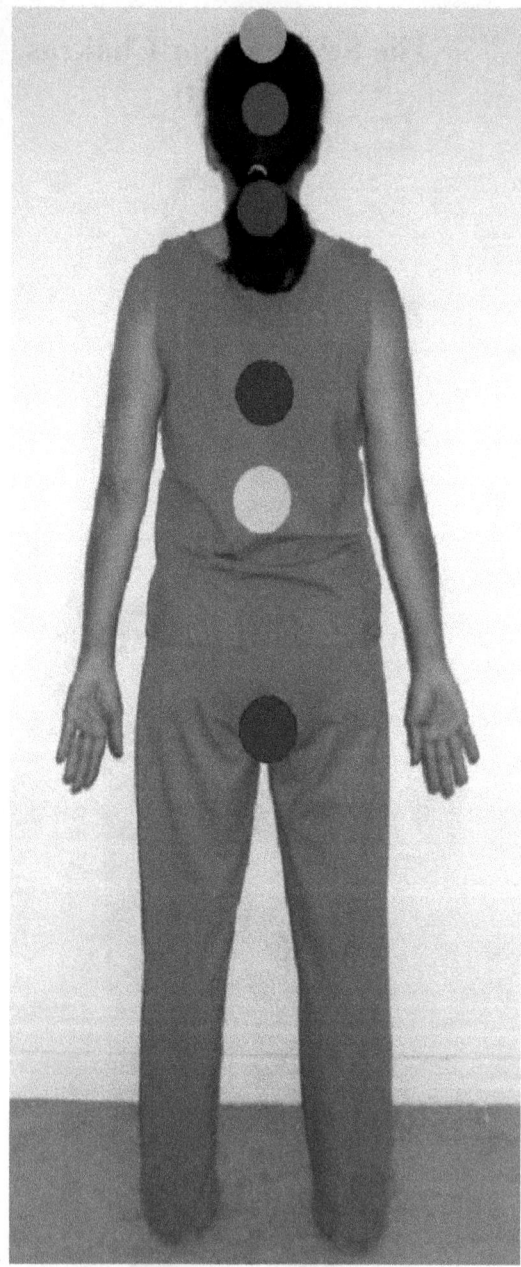

What is a Chakra?

A Chakra is a Sanskrit word meaning, "wheel", or "wheel of light". Each Chakra is seen as spinning in a circular movement and in a specific direction. Each Chakra spins at a different rate of speed. The speed will depend upon many factors such as the health and over all vitality of the individual. The greater the health and vitality, the faster the Chakra spins.

Each Chakra is a center of energy and is recognized to its relationship with the physical, emotional, mental, and spiritual energy systems of the body. Each Chakra has its own name, color, mantra, element, sounds, and more. The whole purpose of studying the Chakra system is to help us integrate wholeness within ourselves.

We can then bring the physical, mental, emotional, and subconscious aspects of health into our lives. We can see that if we feel a certain way, our emotions may actually make us sick. For instance, if you are a very angry person, this anger may translate into a heart condition such as a heart attack.

The Seven Major Chakras are:
1. Root
2. Sacral
3. Solar Plexus
4. Heart
5. Throat
6. Brow
7. Crown

There are several minor chakras:
- **Fingertips**
- **Center of the Palm of the Hands**
- **Center of the Sole of the Feet**

Chakra #1 - The Root

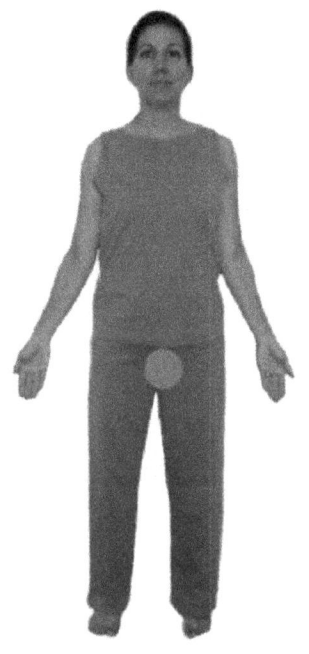

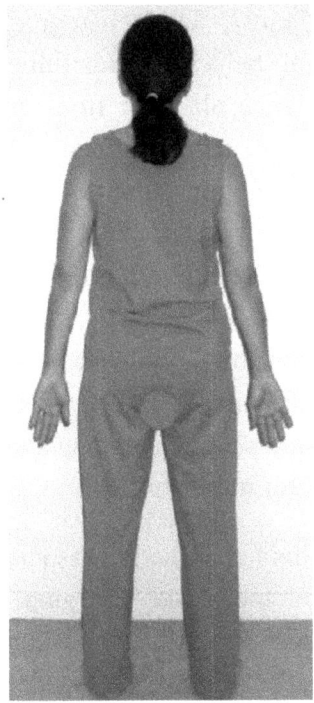

The Root Chakra is also known as the Base Chakra. It is located at the base of the spine (front and back). This chakra governs the adrenal gland and is the sense of smell. This is where physical manifestation happens. The root chakra deals with familial beliefs, superstitions, loyalty, instincts, physical pain, physical pleasure, and the human touch. People who worry about money, food, job security, etc. will have a very inactive or closed chakra area. This chakra is the "right to have".

This chakra includes the base of the spine, coccyges plexus, legs, knees, calves, feet and even the toes. Client's suffering from: obesity, hemorrhoids, constipation, bone disorders, frequent illnesses, fears, inability to focus (grounding), problems of the legs, knees and feet, diarrhea, eating disorders, sciatica, poor circulation, and varicose veins.

This center is associated with the emotions: anger, hatred, self-loathing, racism, revenge, envy sloth, impulsiveness, violent nature, listlessness, edgy, obsessive behaviors, boredom, inaction, giving up, maliciousness, complacency, laziness, autism, dishonesty, insecurity, fear, threat to survival issues, lack of trust or trust issues.

Positive qualities associated with this chakra include: self-esteem, justice and a sense of fair play, love, family, community, gratitude, equality, fortitude, charity, trust, spontaneity, activity, display of leadership skills, ability to be grounded and to be present in the here and now.

Chakra #2 - Sacral

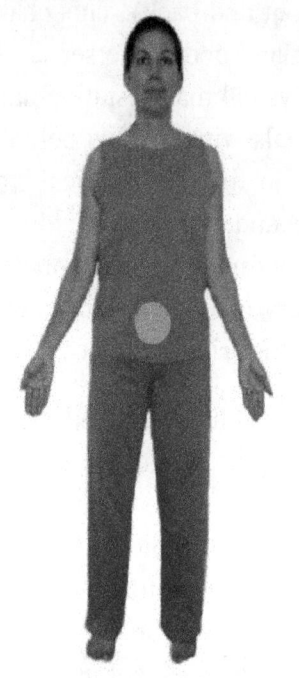

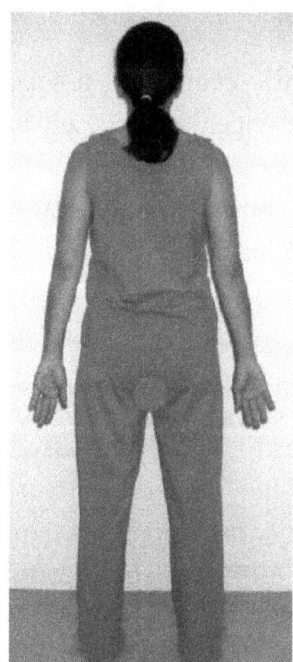

The Second Chakra is called the Sacral Chakra. This chakra is the center for sexual energy and pure emotion. It governs sexuality, creativity, emotions such as anger, fear, and perceptions concerning food and sex. This chakra is our ability and right to feel.

When this chakra is in balance, it provides us with an ease in sharing our emotions with others and sharing the needs of others. We have a positive body awareness of ourselves which results in positive self-esteem. We are able to create and express our individuality and healthy sexuality easily and safely (without harm to others-such as in rape).

When out of balance, one suppresses the expression of natural needs resulting in feelings of inadequacy, possessiveness, jealousy, envy, and self-regret on all levels. Anti-social behaviors, lustfulness, selfishness and arrogance all stem from an imbalance in this chakra center. This center also deals with repressed emotions and inner strength. Other emotions such as the need to control, addictions, shame, guilt, desire, humorlessness, homophobia, disobedience, pride, egoism, sadomasochism, violence, thoughtlessness, hatred, despair of the future, victimization, masochism, sentimentalism, and consumerism (the need for more stuff).

This chakra is associated with the spleen in men and the uterus in women. Impotency, infertility, frigidity, diabetes, kidney problems, bladder problems, reproductive problems, and muscular system problems are all helped with this center.

Chakra #3 - Solar Plexus

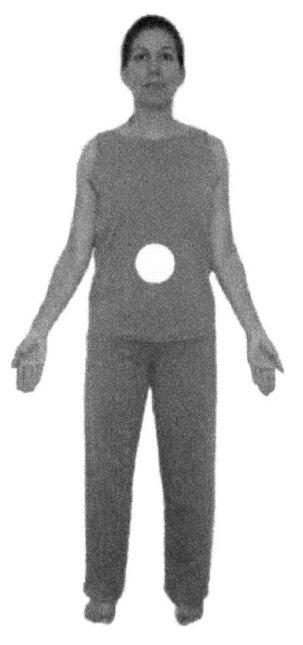

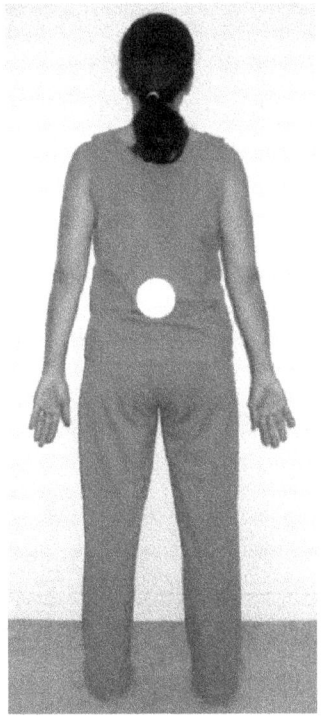

The Third Chakra is known as the Solar Plexus Chakra and is located 2" above the navel. It is where our strength and ability to take action lay. The solar plexus chakra is our personal power center. Our self-motivation stems from this center. Here we make the decisions in our life. This center houses our willfulness and our self-image. It is our sense of sight and the element of fire. Greed, doubt, anger, powerlessness, and guilt are all associated with this center.

When out of balance, one restricts the acceptance of the natural flow of the Universe, creating a need for material reinforcement. Here are the inflated egos, power hungry, your will over others, power, and angers simmer. When properly functioning, one has "gut" instincts of what to do in any given situation.

On a physical level, this chakra deals with issues of food and its assimilation into the body. It deals with how the body digests the food it consumes and distributes it. Here is where digestive problems begin.

The negative attributes of this chakra system include alcoholism, rage, violence, anger, destructive behaviors, bitterness, fury, insecurity, wrath, bickering, passive-aggressive behavior and victimization.

The diseases and illnesses associated with this Chakra include: Ulcers, jaundice, hepatitis, hypoglycemia, gall stones, skin problems, skin diseases, pancreas, nerves, nervous system, pancreas, gall bladder, intestines, and diabetes.

Chakra #4 - Heart

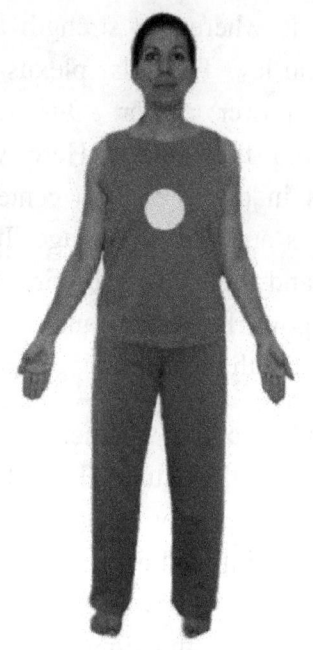

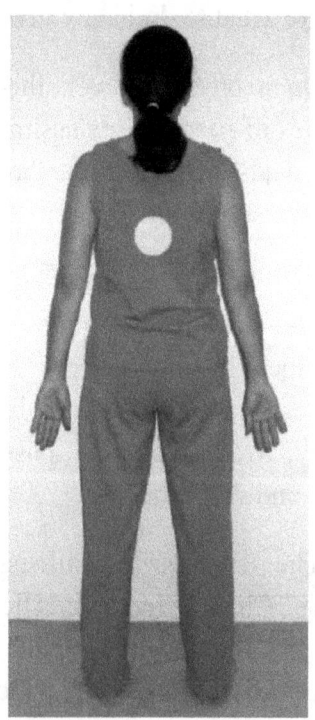

The Fourth Chakra is known as the "Heart Chakra". It is located in the center of the chest and is considered the "center" of the chakra system. This center provides the ability to love freely and unconditionally. A balance between the spiritual and the physical is located here. In the heart chakra our life force in anchored. Through this chakra center, our immune system is strengthened. This center governs the concept of love, how we love, who we love, and why we love. Our compassion stems from this center. It is our sense of touch.

When out of balance we feel restricted in our own ability to give and receive love to both ourselves and to others. Low self-esteem, insecurity, jealousy, feeling unloved, stinginess, self-doubting, "martyr" syndrome, and the "poor me" syndrome are found in this chakra. Betrayal, blame, pessimism, sarcasm, anxiety, perjury, fraud, treachery, deceit, hardness of heart, moral outrage, compassion, mercy, forgiveness, love, satisfaction, gratitude, and also compassion are some of the emotions attached to this chakra center.

This chakra center is also associated with the thymus, heart, blood, circulatory system, glands, lungs, cardiac plexus, and the pericardium. Diseases and ailments connected to this chakra center include: Arthritis, respiratory problem, cardiac problems, stroke, hypertension, nervous headaches, emotional disorders, asthma, allergies, blood pressure, lungs, tissue degeneration, sleep disorders, bronchitis, pneumonia, codependency issues, caretaking issues, relationships, and AIDS.

Chakra #5 - Throat

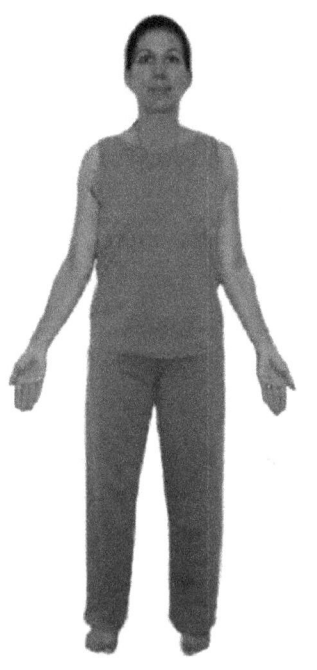

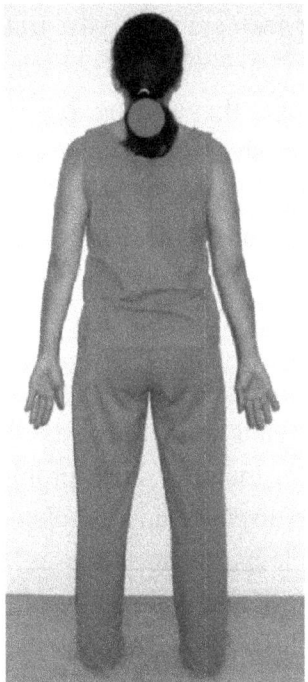

The Fifth Chakra, known as the "Throat Chakra" and it is located at the base of the throat. This chakra allows us to transform our emotions into healthy creative expressions. Here we express ourselves, our beliefs, our feelings and ideas into acceptable forms of communication. It governs our speech, hearing and communication. It is our sense of our own inner voice, our own inner truth. It is the sense of healing and the element of ether.

This chakra empowers us to speak our truth and to allow others their own voice. It governs our telepathy. When in balance, one would feel strength in your convictions, in your truths, in yourself. Organs associated with the throat chakra include: Throat, vocal chords, esophagus, mouth, teeth, thyroid, parathyroid, respiratory system, laryngeal plexus, and the cervical spine.

When out of balance one may have feelings of: fear of judgment or rejection, negative speaking, criticizing, consumerism, addictions and emotional excess. You may suffer from drug addictions, greed of food, greed of things, concealing and/or hiding the truth, obsession, stagnation, lying, hypocrisy, lack of expression, withheld words (biting your tongue), stubborn beliefs, domineering words, and communication problems

Diseases and ailments associated with this energy center include: Sore throats, voice or thyroid problems, flu, vertigo, anemia, allergies, fatigue, asthma, bronchial problems, fevers and laryngitis.

Chakra #6 - Brow

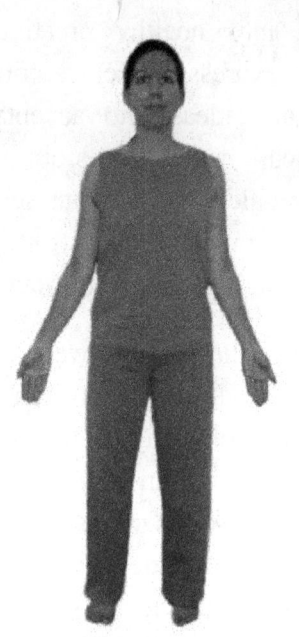

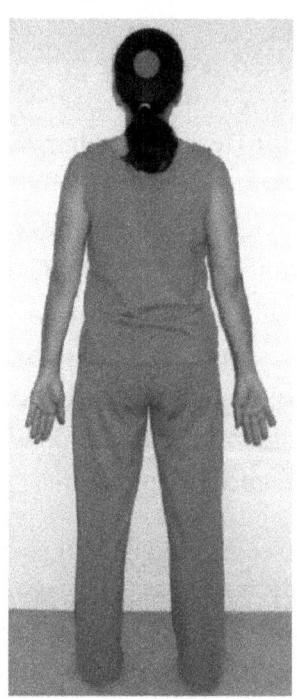

The sixth Chakra is known as the "Brow Chakra" and is located one finger width above the bridge of the nose at the center of the forehead. This center represents the concept of "being" and "existence". This center belongs to the spiritual world. From this center we project our dreams outwards into the physical realm. This is where our source of intuition, insight awareness of self, and clairvoyance stem. It is our physic perception. It is all the elements. The color of this chakra is indigo. When this chakra is out of balance one may experience the following emotions: Self-doubt, injustice, cruelty, inner guilt, forgetfulness, inability to trust our instincts, sadism, ignorance, greed, avarice, stifles wisdom, stifles creativity, stifles prophetic dreams, and superstitious.

When in balance, one would experience emotions such as: creativity, truth, strength, the sharing of ourselves, the sharing of your time with others, the sharing of your needs with others, the sharing of your ideas with others, the sharing of your hopes with others, and the sharing of your fears with others. You will be open to possibilities. You will have a union with the angels in your lives and be more open to the seen, as well as, the unseen.

Organs and ailments associated with this chakra include: sinus problems, congested head, ear diseases and problems, eye diseases and problems, nose diseases and problems, mental problems, head conditions, skeletal system, sleep disorders and problems, pituitary gland, nervous system, pineal gland, headaches, and fuzzy thinking.

Chakra #7 - Crown

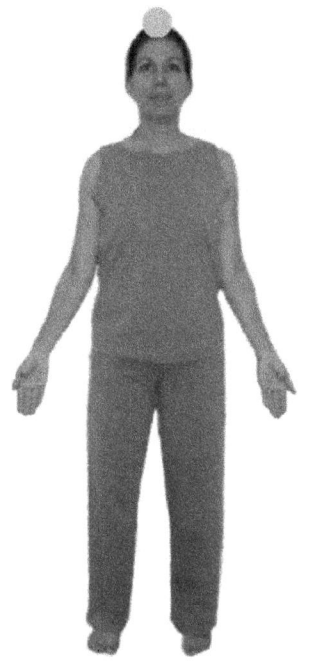

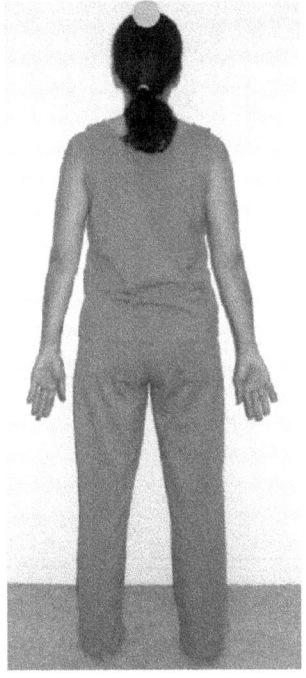

The seventh Chakra is the "Crown Chakra" and is located at the top of the head and slightly to the back. This center allows us to surmount self-limiting thoughts and provides us with the sense of Oneness and Unity with the Divine. It is the connection to the cosmic consciousness, it is spiritual, and it is wisdom. It holds our aspirations and the knowledge of the truth. It reflects our ability to receive light from the source. It is our connection to our higher self and astral travel. It is all the elements, it is cosmic. Through this center we must learn to release, to surrender our will.

When out of balance one would feel emotions such as: anxiety, fear, disconnection with the oneness, feelings of being misunderstood, uninspired, feelings of hatred, gossip, envy, resentments, sorrows, gloom, peer pressure, mob mentality, happy over another's misfortune, self-denial, being impractical and being over imaginative.

When in balance, you would experience emotions such as: Understanding, speaking only words of love and encouragement, taking no pleasure in another's downfall, united to different realms and worlds, lends spiritual support for our journey, spiritual wisdom and interconnectedness.

Ailments and organs associated with this chakra include: insomnia, epilepsy, pain, nervous problems, rheumatism, neuralgia, brain tumors, cerebral tumors, cranial pressure, depression, insanity, confinement, psychosis, worry, and closed mindedness

Earth Chakra

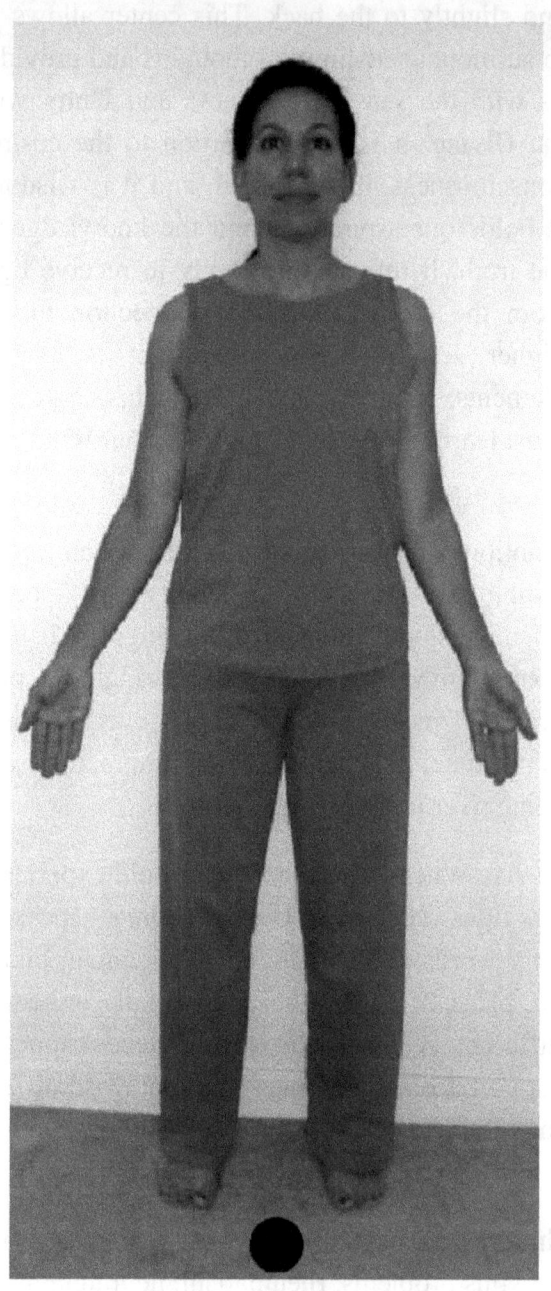

The Earth Chakra is located 10-12" below the feet.

The element is Earth.

The Earth Chakra affects the skeletal system of the body and is associated with the sense of smell.

This chakra affects the physical body in the auric field.

The color of this chakra is brown (all shades) and black.

Ailments associated with this chakra include balance problems, dizziness, grounding, poor circulation, and inability to focus.

When out of balance, the person may feel unstable while walking, unsure of themselves in any situation, autism, fear, lack of trust, insecurity, and laziness.

Positive qualities associated with this chakra include: love, family, community, gratitude, trust, focused, ability to be grounded and to be present in the here and now.

Chapter Six

Byosen, Hibiki and Byosen Reikan-Ho

In Reiki, there is a technique that we can use to access the condition of our client. It is called **Byosen Reikan-Ho**. The word **Byosen** is two words, "*Byo*" and "*sen*." '*Byo*' means disease, toxic, illness or sickness and *sen* means precedence, gland or mass.' Loosely translated, Byosen means 'mass of disease' or 'gland of sickness.' The word Reikan is also two words where 'Rei' represents spirit or universal and 'kan' means sensation or feeling. 'Ho' means work. If we put this all together, Byosen Reikan-Ho means 'working with the sensation (or universal feeling) of an area of disease or sickness.'

We can detect lumps, masses, and areas of blockages through a technique called "*Scanning*." Scanning is the process of passing our hands over the body to detect energy signals (sensations). These sensations are a way for us to understand what is happening in the body and shows us areas that are in need of Reiki energy. We can call these sensations, '*Hibiki*.' Hibiki is a Japanese word that means resonance or 'echo.' It is pronounced (He-bi-ki). Our body is sending out an echo of what is happening inside of it. Much like our modern day sonograms that send sound into the body and technicians measure the waves as they bounce off the organs, tumors, cysts, etc., inside of our body.

When we pass our hands over a client, the areas of the client that are in need of Reiki energy will give off a sensation (Hibiki) that we will be able to perceive through our hands. Each Reiki practitioner is unique and so is their perception of these sensations.

Hibiki

- **Extra Warmth**-To me, when I feel warmth, this is an area that needs Reiki energy. I will give Reiki energy at this point until the warmth feels balanced.
- **Intense Warmth**-This is an area that is in desperate need of Reiki energy. I will send Reiki until the area felt balanced.
- **Tingling**-While some people access energy as tingling in their hands, to me it represents an area of inflammation. The amount of inflammation that I feel will tell me how acute or chronic the inflammation in.
- **Repulsion-(Repelling)**-An area that does not want Reiki energy (or has had enough Reiki energy) and is now pushing you away from it.
- **Ebb/Tide**-or flux and flow pattern is a good thing. This indicates that the energy system is balanced and is in good working order. You can still give this client a Reiki treatment if you want.
- **Pain**-An area that has a blockage or build-up of excess. Sometimes this may signify a referral to another system in the body.

- **Attraction-(Magnetism)-** Area is in need of Reiki energy that-pulls you in.
- **Coldness-** When I feel an area that is cold or cool, it represents an emotional blockage. Most of the time the client does not want me to work on this area as they are not ready to release the situation. To other practitioners, sensing coolness or coldness signifies an area that is in need of energy due to an energy blockage. Some practitioners will stay with their hand position on this area until it becomes warm.

When we refer to masses or lumps, we are also referring to an accumulation of energy in the form of either physical ailments or to a build-up of negative emotions. In this way, you may sense an imbalance in an area where physical pain exists or where there is an excess of anger. Any accumulation in the body will act like a kink in the garden hose. When you turn the garden hose on and the hose is open-water runs freely through it, but when the hose is closed (or if there is a kink in it), water may have trouble passing through it easily and freely. In this example, water symbolizes both the blood and the energy of the body. Since blood carries with it many nutrients (like oxygen), if it cannot get to the muscle, organs and tissues then those areas may start to starve and become sick or die. So it is also with energy. When energy becomes stuck or stagnant, it keeps other areas of the body from receiving vital energy and health.

Byosen Reikan-Ho

When you scan your own energy system, this is called Byosen Reikan-Ho.

Assignment:
Take your hand and place them 1-2" off your body with palms of the hands facing your body. Now, starting at the top of your head slowly pass your hands over the front of your body. Make an assessment of your chakra.

How to do Body Scanning on Table
1. Position both of your hands 1-2" above the physical body of your client.
2. Starting above your client's head, slowly move your hands down their body to their below their feet and back up their body returning to your starting position 1-2" above your client's head.
3. Repeat this scanning technique when you turn your client over.

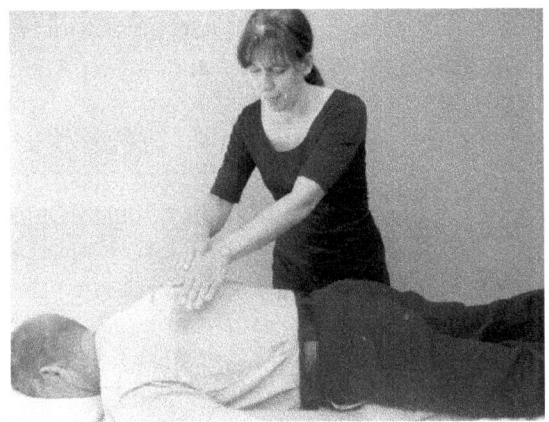

What you are doing is gathering information on the energy signature that the client's body is giving off. As you were passing your hands slowly down the client's body, did you feel areas of intense heat, or cold? Did you feel dips and valleys? Did you feel tingling sensations? Were you drawn into certain areas and repelled at other areas? Do not become discouraged if you feel nothing at all after a body scan. With practice and patience, you will begin to notice the subtle changes in the auric field. You will also learn what certain sensations mean in the body.

Exercise to See an Aura:

In this exercise, you will experience seeing your aura, the life force energy that surrounds all living things. To do this you will rub your hands briskly together once again. Focus your mind on your hands. Now place your hands, palms facing you above your head. Have the fingers of both hands facing each other and keep them about 1/2 inches apart. It is also helpful if the ceiling behind your hands is white. Now, allow your eyes to go out of focus and just lazily stare at the space between the tips of your middle fingers. In time, you will be able to see a haze appear around your fingers. This haze will be translucent or opaque in appearance. This is your life force energy. With practice, you will also begin to see a second layer form. This layer has a jagged edge and is blue in color. This is a layer of your aura. Do not be too hard on yourself if you did not see anything while trying this exercise. With patience and practice you will succeed:

When working with Reiki energies we can significantly alter and modify the layers of energy that surround each and every one of us. Reiki works on ALL levels for healing, both inside our bodies dealing with physical, emotional and mental healing, as well as, outside of our bodies dealing with the many layers of our aura (our first defense against disease and illness).

Aura Scanning

Remember we talked about the energy that surrounds us all? This is called the aura. The aura is made up of many layers and many colors. I am only bringing this up so that you may be aware that you can use the same techniques you used for body scanning for scanning the aura as well.

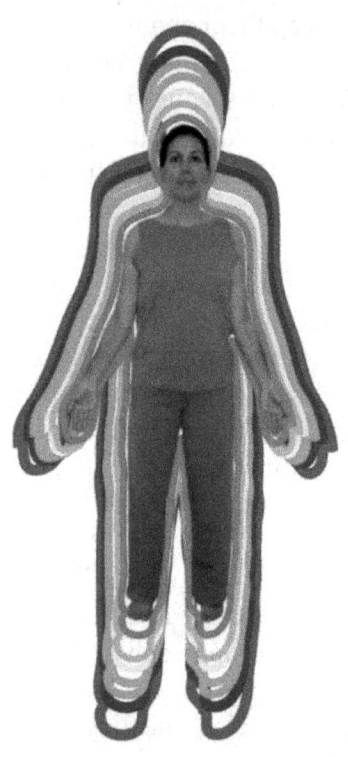

To scan the aura, you will lift both your hands about 3' off your client's body. I slowly and deliberately begin lowering both of hands and stop 2" above the client's body. When I reach that point, I lift my hands off the body and shake them out. Then I lift both of my hands again 3' above the client's body and this time I am in a new location.

I continue to lower my hands through the layers of the aura, and when I reach 2" above the client's body, I remove my hands and shake them out. I like to start at the head of the client and work down to the feet.

The most important thing to do is to go slowly. Sometimes if you close your eyes, you will be more focused on the energy that your fingers are sensing. But ultimately, it will take practice. The more you practice, the more sensitive you will become and the better able you will become at picking up the little differences in energy sensations. So practice!

You will be surprised at some of the sensations you may feel in the aura. You may encounter shapes of substance, tingling sensations, warmth, coldness, holes and tears. There are many books out on the market with techniques on dealing with balancing the aura. One note here is this, Reiki was never taught to work in the aura.

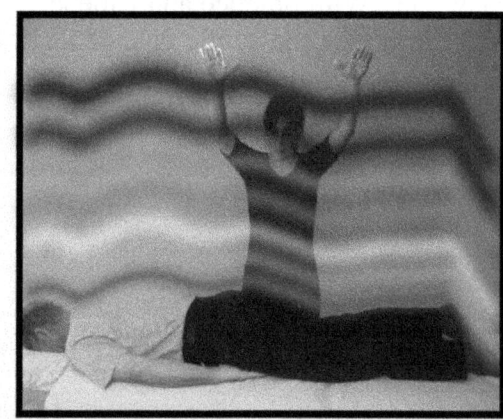
#1
Begin as high as you can comfortably extend your arms

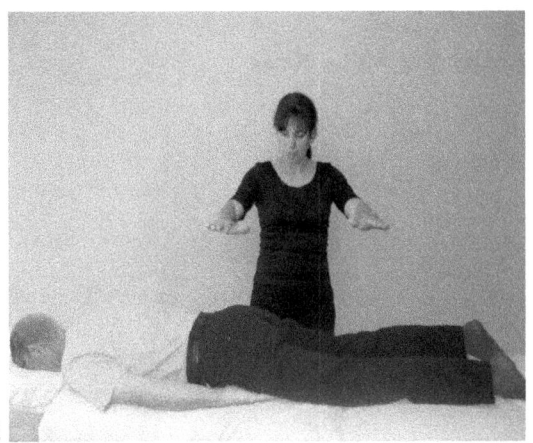

#2
Slowly allow your hands to fall down through the auric layers

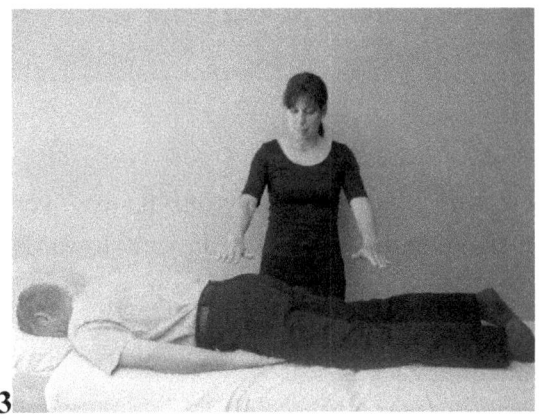

#3
Stop your hands about 1"- 2" above your client's body

Assignment:
Find a willing volunteer and have them lie, or sit, in a comfortable position. Begin with your hand 3' above their body and slowly bring your hand to 1"-2" above their physical body. Lift your hands off the body and repeat in another area of the body. I like to start at the top of the head and move down the body for a total of at least 10 passes.

Chapter Seven
Hand Positions for Healing Yourself

Using the Hand Positions for Healing Yourself

Before you begin this, or any other energy work session, be sure to use a grounding meditation. You can use the one that I have listed in an earlier chapter, or create one that feels right to you.

Stay on each hand position for 3 to 5 minutes each. Allow your intuition to guide you. If you think that you need to stay on a place for a longer period of time, then please do so. If you feel the need to move on more quickly, then do that. Each session will be unique. These hand positions would be a great way to calm an anxious client before their regular massage (or other) session and it can be performed while the client is in the seated position.

Be sure to breathe regularly in through your nose and out through your mouth. To enhance the energy flow, you can place the tip of your tongue on the roof of your mouth and contract your Hui Yin point (something that we will discuss in future levels).

Position 1 - The Top of the Head

Position 2 - The Eyes

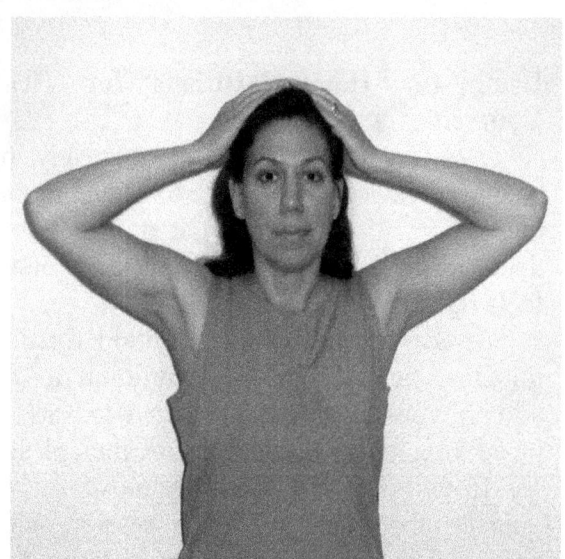

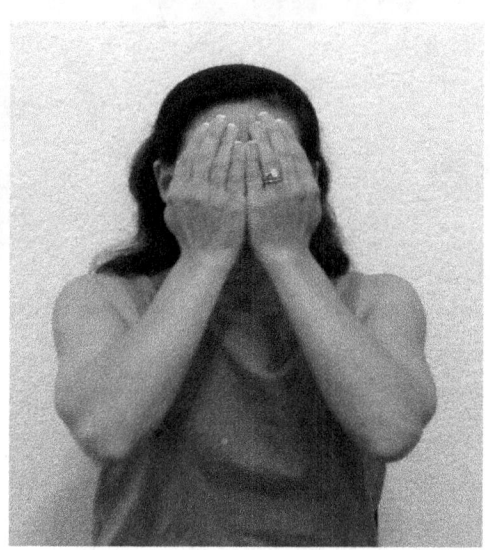

To Do: Place both hands, palms down, gently on the top of your head. Allow the tips of your middle fingers to touch each other. Close your eyes and take a nice, slow, and deep breath in through your nose. Try to imagine that you are breathing in both oxygen and Reiki energy at the same time. As you breathe in, you allow the energy to enter your body and flow through your body, through your arms, to your hands, out your hands, into your head.

Stay here for 3-5 minutes. This is your Pineal gland. This is where we feel our connectedness to the oneness of the Universe (God, source, Great Spirit, Etc.)

To Do: Place both of your hands over your eyes, with palms facing inward towards your eyes. Your fingers should be positioned so that the fingertips of your middle fingers are touching each other.

This position is the Pituitary Gland and will help those who are suffering from sinus problems, congestion in the head, headaches, eye problems and diseases, mental problems, head problems, nose problems and diseases, fuzzy thinking, the skeletal system, and the nervous system.

Position 3 - The Ears

To Do: Place the palm of your hands on either side of the jaw and ears with your fingertips pointing towards the back of your head. Close your eyes and take a deep breath imagining both oxygen and Reiki energy entering your body, flowing through your arms, into your hands, out your hands, and into your ears and surrounding area.

Use this area for ear problems and diseases, to reduce stress held in the jaw, TMJ, mouth and tongue problems, gum problems, teeth problems, hearing problems, deafness, ringing in the ear, eardrum damage, and swimmer's ear.

Position 4 - Back of the Head

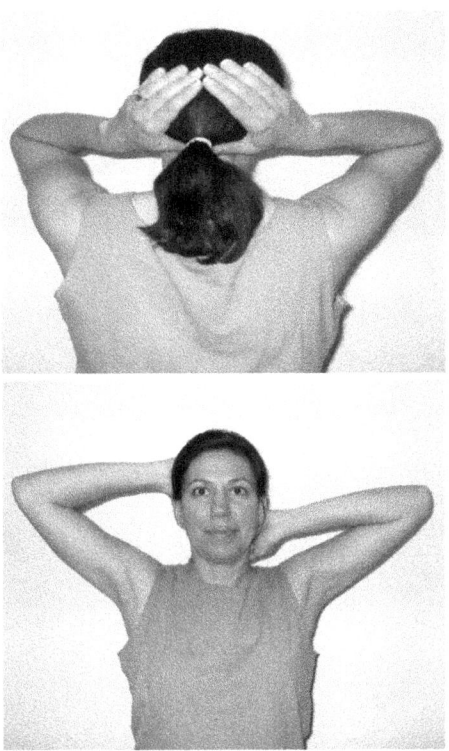

To Do: Cup your hands and place them under the lower portion of the skull and cradle your head. Close your eyes and breathe in the Reiki energy with the oxygen and feel the energy flow through your body, through your arms, through your hands and into the back of your head.

This position will help with people who suffer from headaches and migraines, tension and stress, fuzzy thinking, anxiety, head injuries, and head problems.

Head Position 5 - Throat

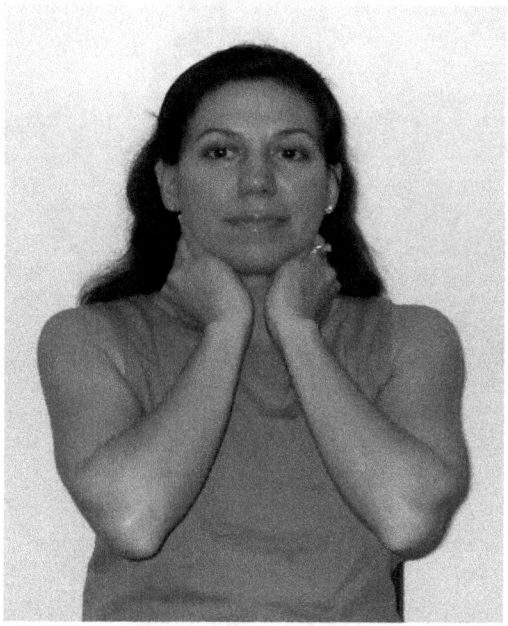

To Do: Place both of your cupped hands on your throat area with the heels of your hands touching each other. You fingers are pointed towards the back of your neck. Close your eyes and imagine breathing in both oxygen and Reiki energy. Feel the Reiki energy flow through your arms, through your hands and into your neck area.

Use this position for throat problems and diseases, vocal cords, esophagus, mouth problems and diseases, teeth problem and diseases, thyroid, respiratory system, addictions, laryngeal plexus, cervical spine, and parathyroid.

Position 6 - Heart

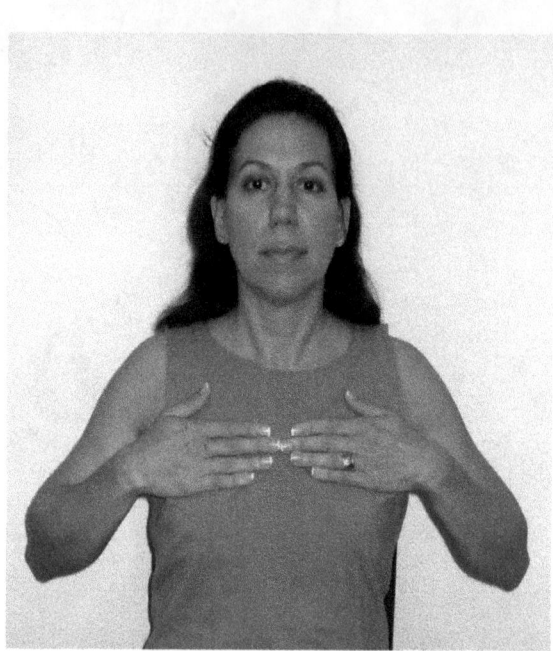

To Do: Place your hands over the chest area. When working on a female client, you should NEVER place your hands directly on their breasts. In some states, it is not only immoral; it is illegal to do so. You can place your hands 2-4" above the heart area and send Reiki energy into that area.

This position will help those suffering from cardio-vascular problems, arthritis, stroke, hypertension, blood pressure, lung problems and diseases, asthma, allergies, bronchitis pneumonia, AIDS, circulatory system, thymus, heart problems and diseases, blood problems and diseases, gland problems and diseases.

Hand Position 7 - The Solar Plexus

Position 8 - Spleen

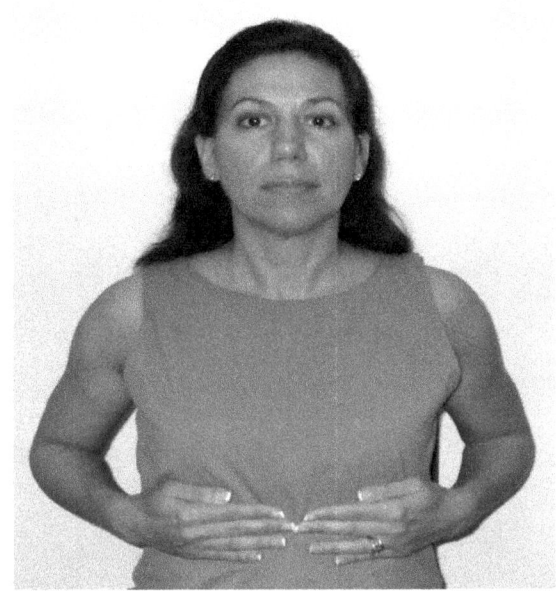

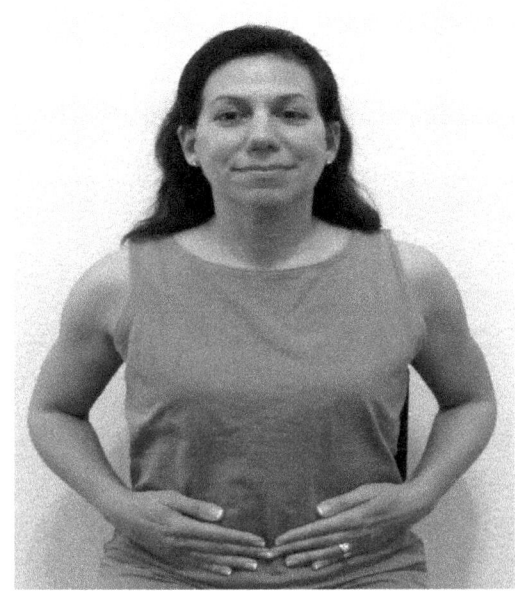

To Do: Place your hands over the solar plexus area with your fingertips pointing towards each other. The middle fingers may touch if you wish to. This position will help those who are suffering from stomach problems and diseases, liver problems and diseases, level of sugar in the blood, Spleen problems and diseases, pancreas problems and diseases, gall bladder problems and diseases, small intestine problems and diseases, assimilation of food in the body, adrenal problems and diseases, solar plexus, and the digestive system. This is our Seat of Personal Power. Our self-motivation stems from this area. Greed, doubt, anger, powerlessness, and guilt all stem from this area.

To Do: Place your hands on your spleen area. This area will help those who are suffering from Spleen problems and diseases, large intestine problems and diseases, small intestine and diseases, traverse colon problems and diseases, digestive problems and diseases, elimination problems and diseases, constipation, diarrhea, flatulence, womb, urinary problems and diseases, the urinary tract, and problems with the navel.

This area will also people who are suffering from diabetes, infertility, impotence, kidney problems and diseases, muscular system problems, gonads, fallopian tubes, and reproductive problems and diseases.

Position 9 - Base Chakra - Groin Area

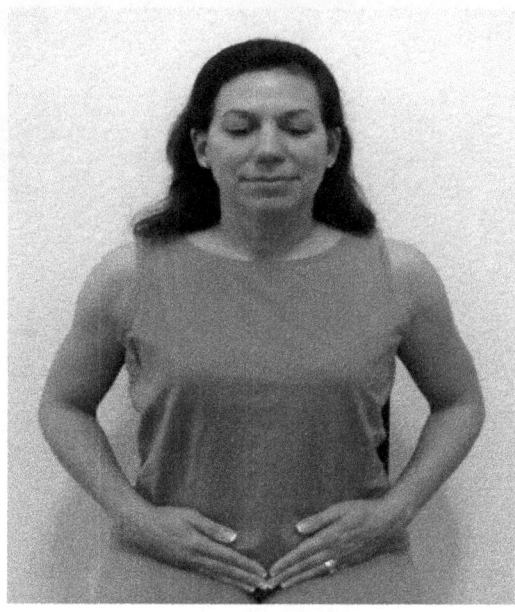

To Do: Place your hands on the base area of your body (where the pubic bone is) with your fingertips pointing downward towards the ground and the thumbs and index fingers touching (if you so desire). Breathe in Reiki energy with the oxygen and feel the Reiki energy flow down through your arms, through your hands and into the groin area.

This position will help those who suffer from groin pulls, groin problems and diseases, ilium muscle, and sexual problems and diseases.

Hand Position 10 - Adrenals

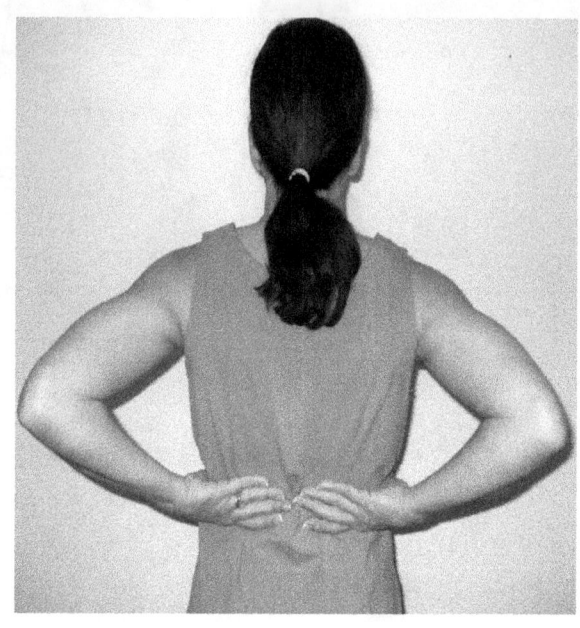

To Do: Place your hands on your back as high up as you can comfortably reach them. The fingertips of your hands should be pointing in towards each other. If this position is too uncomfortable for you, then you can skip this hand position. Breathe in oxygen mixed with Reiki energy and feel the Reiki energy flowing through your body, down your arms, through your hands and into your adrenals and the adrenal area.

This hand position will help those who are suffering from adrenal problems and diseases including low energy and low metabolism.

Hand Position 11 - Lower Back

Hand Position - 12 - Tailbone

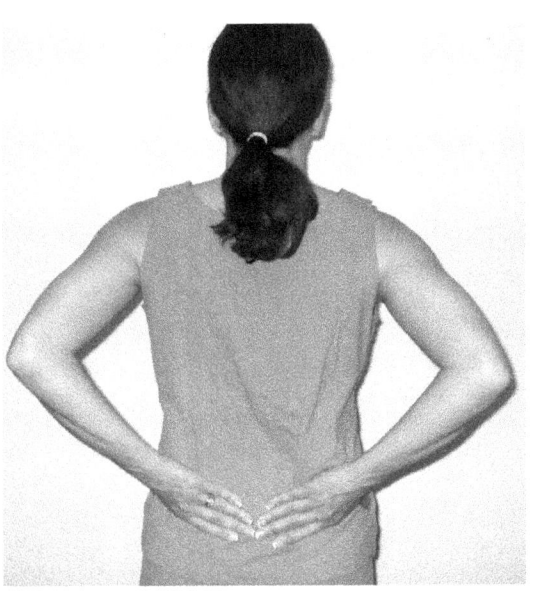

To Do: Place your hands on your lower back. It is not necessary for the fingertips of your hands to be touching. Breathe in the Reiki energy and feel it flow down your arms, through your hands and into the lower back area.

This position will help those suffering from lower back problems and diseases, disc problems and diseases, spine problems and diseases, sciatica, digestive problems and diseases, intestinal problems and diseases, constipation, diarrhea, elimination problems and diseases, kidney problems and diseases, skeletal system, elimination system, urinary problems and diseases, reproductive problems and diseases, poor circulation and obesity.

To Do: Place your hands over the center line of your spine with the fingertips of your hands pointing downward. It is not necessary to have your fingers touching.

This hand position will help those who are suffering from back problems and diseases, sciatica, disk problems and diseases, kidney problems and diseases, leg problems and diseases, poor circulation, skeletal system, constipation, diarrhea, elimination problems and diseases, urinary problems and diseases, varicose veins, hemorrhoids, bone disorders, and frequent illnesses.

Hand Position 13 – Knees

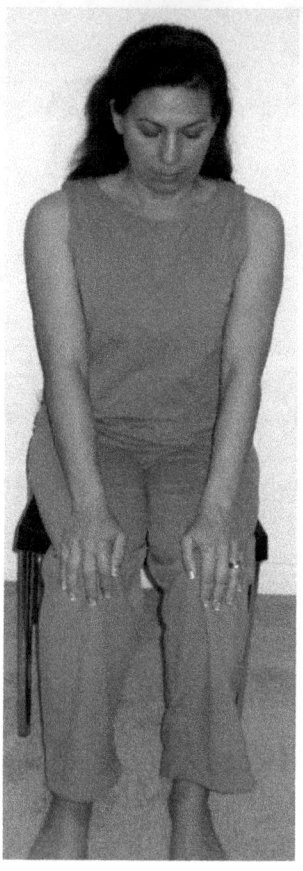

Hand Position 14 - The Ankle

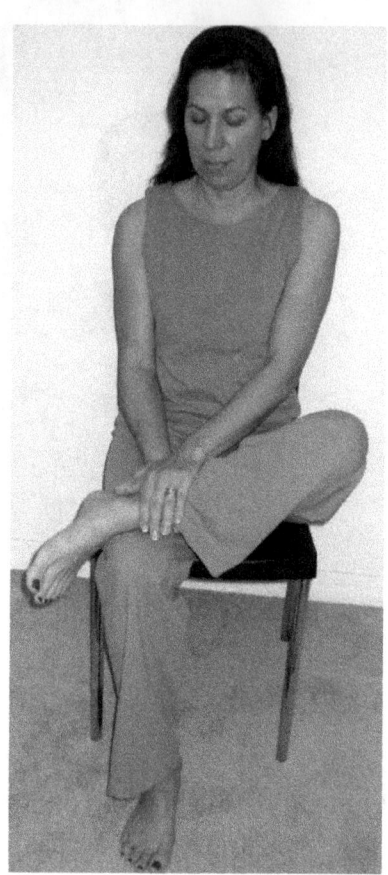

To Do: Place the palm of your right hand on your right knee and the palm of your left hand on your left knee. Breathe in the Reiki energy and feel the energy flow down through your arms, flow through your hands and into the knee and knee area of your body.

This position will help those suffering from knee problems/diseases, leg problems/diseases, sciatica, poor circulation, varicose veins, and problems of the skeletal system. The knee is also associated with the digestive system.

To Do: Place your right hand on your right ankle and your left hand on your left ankle. Breathe in Reiki energy and feel the energy flow down through your arms, flow through your hands and into your ankles.

This hand position will help those who are suffering from ankle problems and diseases, feet problems and diseases, leg problems and diseases, poor circulation, sciatica, varicose veins, bone disorders, and the skeletal system.

Hand Position #15 - The Foot

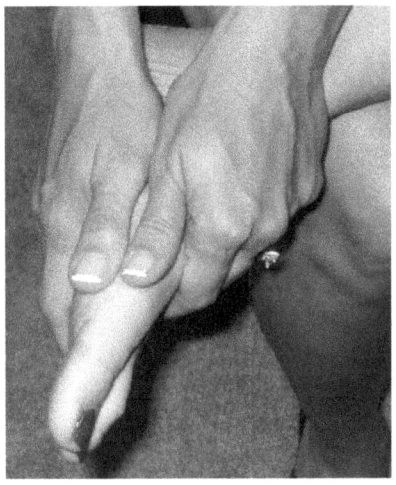

To Do:

In this position we are using the technique called "sandwiching". This is where both of our hands are surrounding a particular area of the client's body. The Sandwiching hand position works excellent on joint areas such as the elbows, wrists, knees and ankles. I also use it for the hands and feet. This position will help those who suffer from feet problems, varicose veins, circulation problems, and skeletal problems.

Chapter Eight
Hand Positions for Healing Others

Just like the hand positions discussed earlier in the book, we will now discuss some basic hand positions that you will use in the typical Reiki healing session. Reiki practitioners begin the healing session by sitting at the head of their client. Beginning at the top of the head, the Reiki practitioner will work down the client's body, ending at their feet. When completed, the Reiki practitioner will then ask the client to turn over.

The Reiki practitioner will then continue with the Reiki hand positions starting once again at the client's head and working down their body, ending at their feet. When placing your hands on your body, be sure you are gentle and loving. Keep your hands in one hand position for approximately three minutes before moving on to the next hand position. If you feel an area needs more time-give it to it.

You can light a candle and play music to help make this time special to you and your client.

Remember-NEVER touch your client's private areas.

Hand Positions for the Front of the Body

Position One – Crown Chakra

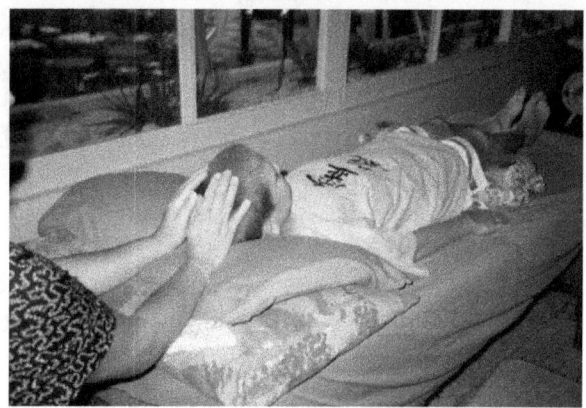

With client lying face up, sit (or stand) behind the client and place both of your hands on the client's head. In the picture above, I am placing my hands with thumbs touching and fingers pointing upwards. I am sending Reiki energy into the client's head first and then, through my intention, I am sending Reiki energy down through the head to the client's body.

Use this position for imbalances in the head due to headaches and head injuries. This position will help with stress. Use this position for the pineal and hypothalamus gland. This position will help to improve motor (and thinking) functions.

Position Two - Brow Chakra (Front)

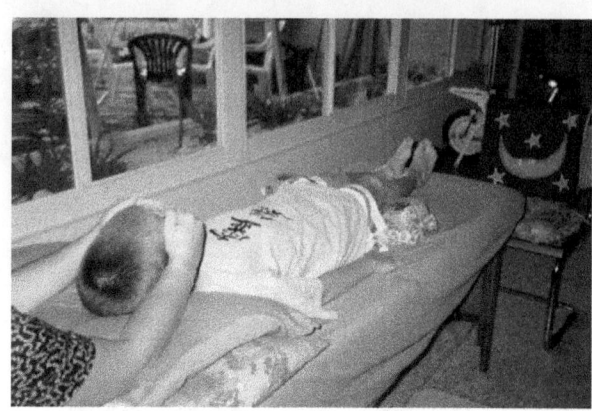

Cover your client's face with a tissue and place your hands on their face. This position will help with imbalances of the thalamus and pituitary glands, eyes and sinus problems, headaches, allergies, hay fever, and mouth, gum, and teeth problems.

Position Three – Throat Chakra

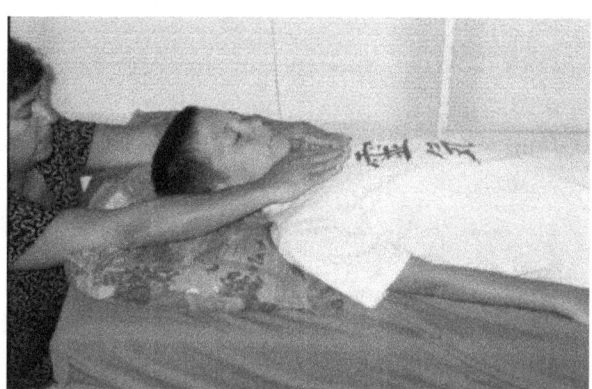

Place your hands above your client's throat area. Do not lay your hands on the client's throat area. This position helps the immune system, metabolism and throat problems. Also included are calcium absorption, weight control, and energy

42

stimulator.

Position Four – Heart Chakra

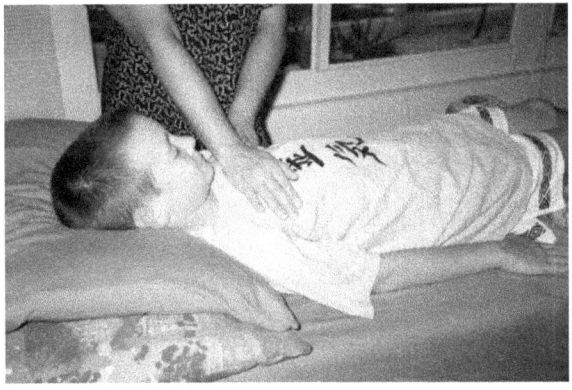

Place your hands on the heart area. If working on a female client, DO NOT place your hands on her chest but rather above it. This position helps imbalances in the lymph system. Tumors, cysts, headaches, breast problems including lactation, and PMS, are all helped by this center.

Position Five - Solar Plexus Chakra

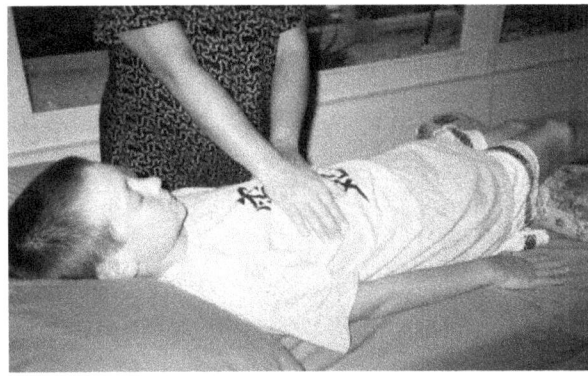

This position is located at the base of the rib cage and above the navel. Place your hands on this area for all digestive and stomach problems, and imbalances in blood sugar levels (such as diabetes), spleen, liver, gall bladder, and the pancreas. Constipation problems will also be helped with this area.

Position Six – Spleen Chakra (Front)

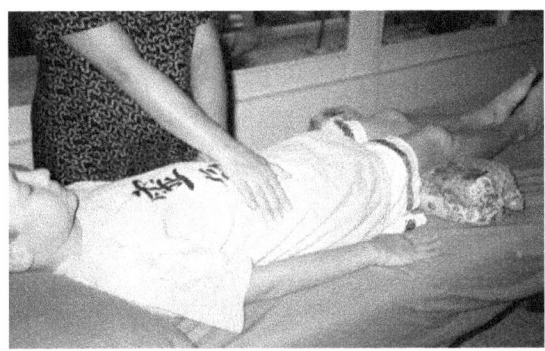

Place your hands on the sacral area located just below the navel. This hand position will help with imbalances in the menstrual cycle, the bladder, infections, arthritis, migraines and headaches, ovaries, cysts, lower intestines, colon, the adrenal and pineal glands, and all vaginal or uterus disorders.

Position Seven – Knees

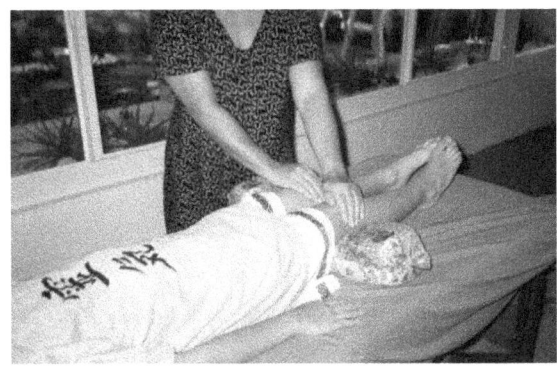

Place your hands gently on your client's knees.. Use this position to help all knee, leg, ankle, and foot problems including sciatica and varicose veins. This position will also help with blood circulation.

Position Eight – Ankles

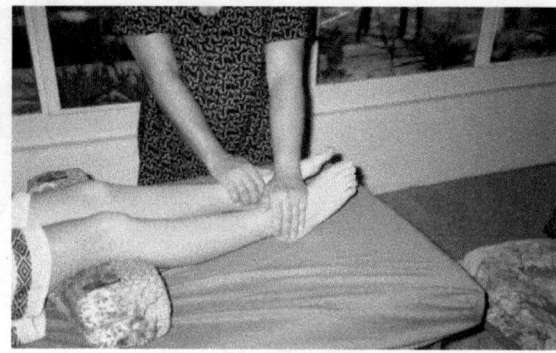

Place your hands gently on your client's ankles. This position will help with all ankles and feet problems including swollen ankles and varicose veins. Use this position for circulation problems, anterior tibia's problems, and shin splints.

Position Nine - Feet

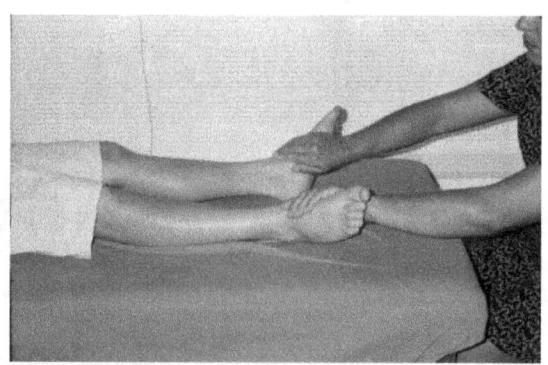

Place your hands on the inside of your client's feet as shown above. Use this position for all foot problems including corns. Other conditions helped by this hand position are; stress, and circulatory problems.

Position Ten - Bottom of Feet

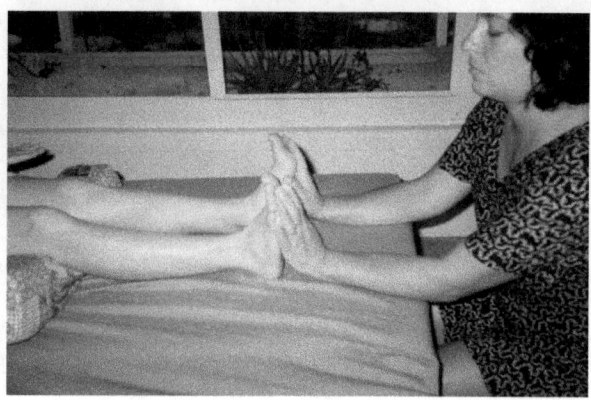

Place your hands on the bottom of your client's feet with your fingers pointing upwards toward your client's toes. In this position I first send Reiki energy into the client's foot, and then I imagine the energy flowing up the client's leg, up the torso and up through and out of the head. I see the energy being accepted by the client's body and pushing all illnesses and dis-harmony out, as well as, to remove negative energies and other toxins from the client's body.

NOTES:

Hand Positions for the Back of Body

Position 11 – Brow Chakra (Back)

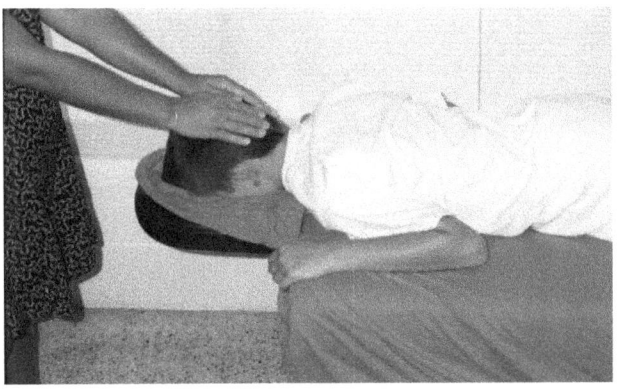

Place your hands on your client's head. Use this position for imbalances in the Pineal and Hypothalamus gland. This position will help people who are suffering from headaches and head injuries, stroke, eye problems, nose bleeds, and other eye and nose problems.

Position 12 – Throat Chakra

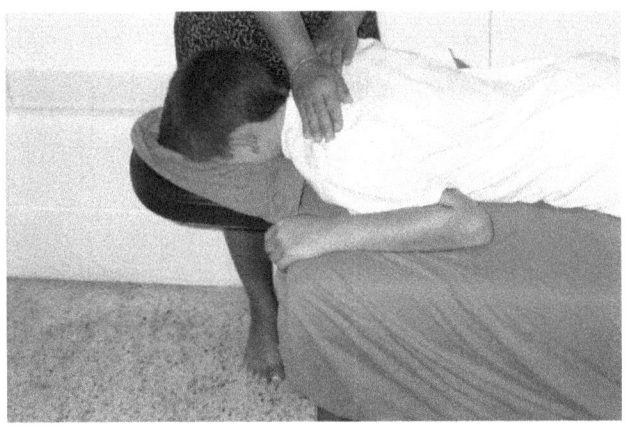

Place hands on the bottom of the neck (upper back area). Use this hand position for client's who suffer from throat problems, stress and tension, spinal problems and headaches.

Position 13 – Heart Chakra

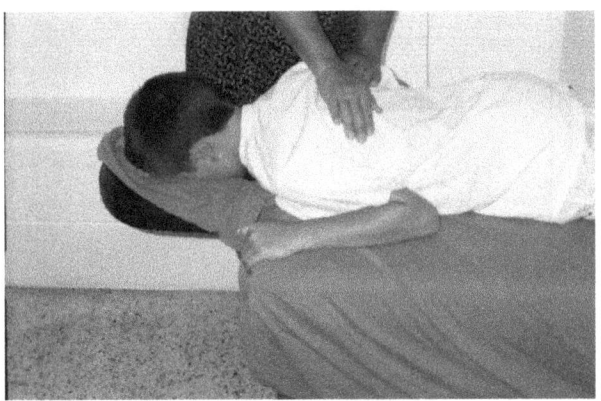

Place your hands over the heart area located between the lower scapula area and center of the rib cage. Use this position to treat all heart and lung problems.

Position 14 - Solar Plexus Chakra

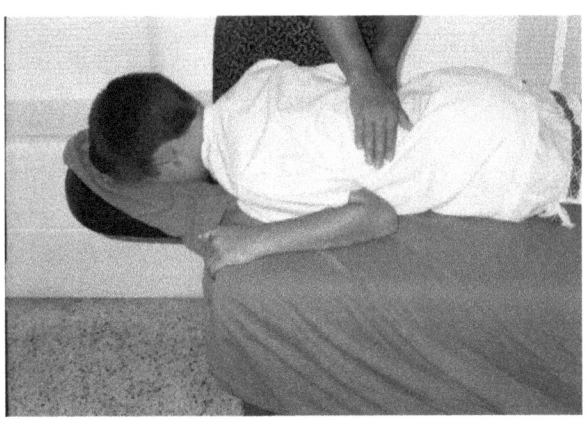

Place your hands on the solar plexus area located right over the adrenals, just below the ribcage but above the navel. This hand position will help diabetes, hypoglycemia, hyperglycemia, migraines, stress, tension, male and female reproductive problems.

Position 15 - Spleen Chakra

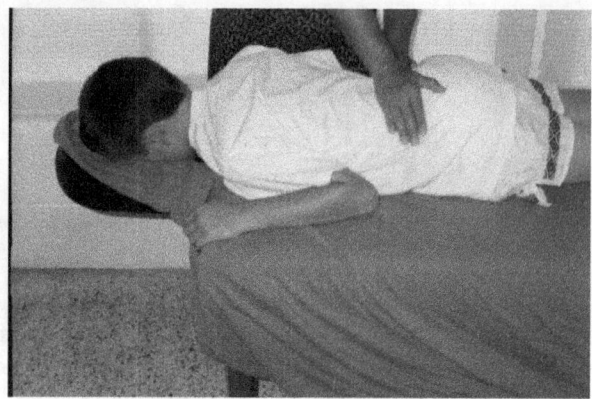

Place your hands on the client's spleen area located below the waistline. This position will help kidney problems, spleen, edema, infections, high blood pressure, and arthritis.

Position 16 - Root Chakra

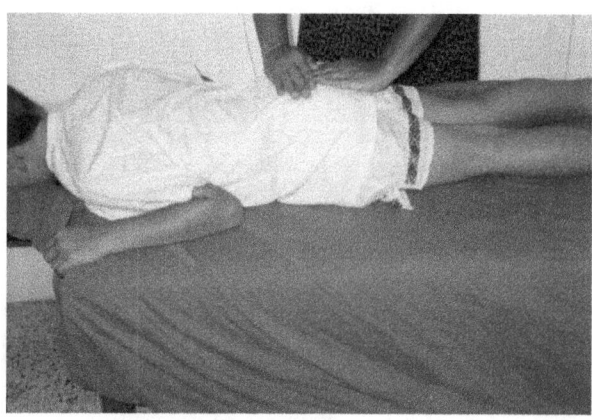

Place your hands over the coccyx area located at the base of the spine, the tailbone. This position will help clients who suffer from intestinal disorders, lower back problems, lumbar problems and disorders, and sacral disorders. This also includes sciatic problems.

Position 17 - Back of Knees

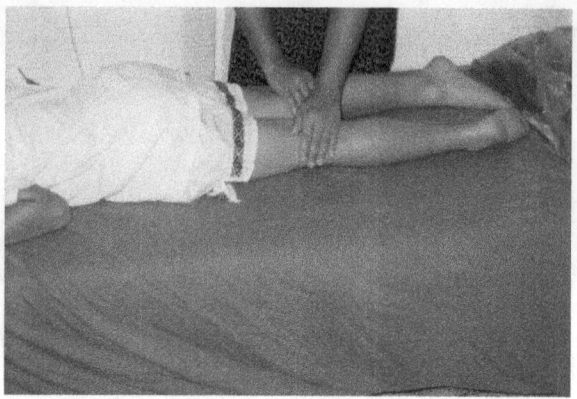

Place your hands gently on the backs of their knees. Do not add pressure to your hands. Use this hand position to help clients who suffer from Sciatic nerve problems, varicose veins, circulation in the legs, and knee injuries.

Position 18 - Back of Ankles (Back)

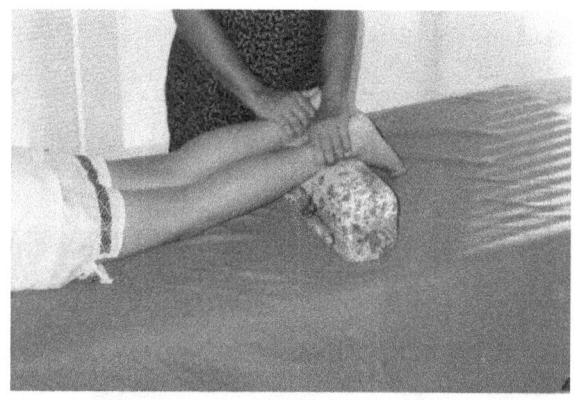

Place your hands on the client's ankles.. This hand position will help clients who suffer from sciatic nerve problems, circulation in the legs and feet, varicose veins, edema, and ankles problems

Position 19 - Bottoms of Feet

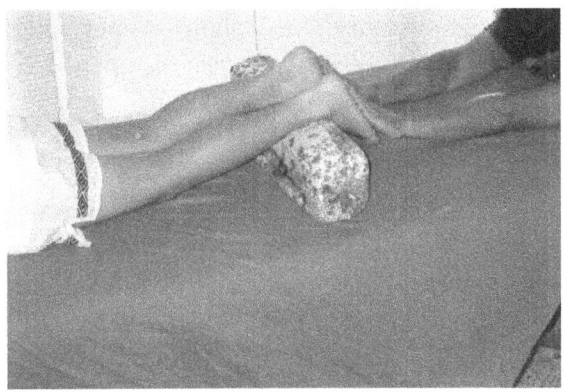

Place your hands on your client's feet as shown above. Plant your feet on the ground, be sure you are grounded. Now, you can do the following:

1. Send energy into the soles of the feet.
2. Now you can "push" Reiki energy up through the legs and out of the client's crown chakra (top of the head) to help remove any additional blockages of energy that is in the body.
3. You can also pull the energy down from the client's crown chakra (top of head), down their body, down their legs, and into their feet. I then draw that energy through my own hands, through my body, and down into my feet where I send it into the earth. (I send it into the earth to be transmuted into love.)

This hand position will help clients who are suffering from sciatic nerve problems, circulation in the legs and feet, varicose veins, feet problems, and grounding issues and blockages.

Closing the Session

Methods and Techniques

There are many ways in which Reiki practitioners may choose to close their Reiki sessions. Below is a list of some commonly used ways to "close" the Reiki session.

- **Angel Wings**
- **Cocoon**
- **Spinal ZigZag**

Angel Wings

In performing the angel wings closing technique, you will stand facing your client on either side of the massage table. Your client will have their face down in the face cradle during this time. Begin by placing both of your hands on the upper back of your client. You will then do a wide sweeping motion to the outside of the client (towards the client's shoulder) and then sweep your hands down to the clients' lower spine.

You are imitating the "wings of an angel". When you reach the lower spine, you will lift your hands off the client's body and place them once again at the top of the client's back and sweep your hands down the client's body to the lower spine. Repeat for a total of three complete sweeps.

Note: you should do this exercise with caution. Don't be rough.

You are just gently and lovingly sweeping your hands over the client's body. Some people will barely feel the movement because you are doing this so gently. If you do not want to (or can't) touch the person's body, then this whole exercise may be down 2-4" above the client's body. It is a nice finishing touch either way.

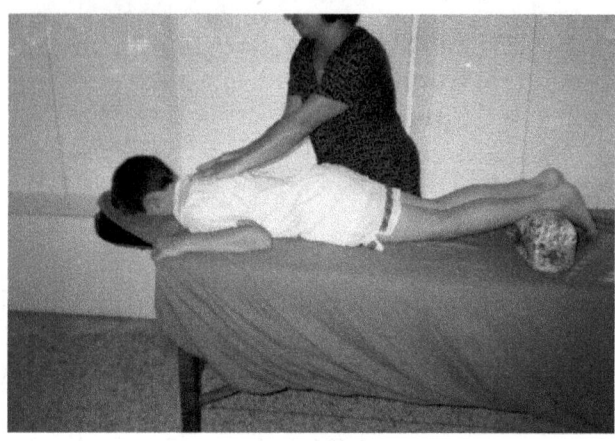

Angel Wings

The Cocoon

While working on a client's energy field, you have probably opened up their Chakra systems. Never allow your clients to leave with their Chakra systems opened. This is one technique I use to close down each Chakra.

When finished with the session, take both of your hands and imagine circling your client and placing them into a large cocoon. I do a sweeping motion with my arms around the client as I stand off to the side of the table. Do the sweeping motion for a total of three times.

When finished, visualize the client in a safe and loving cocoon and fill that cocoon with Reiki energy. Tap them on their shoulder (to signify the session is over) and say "Thank you".

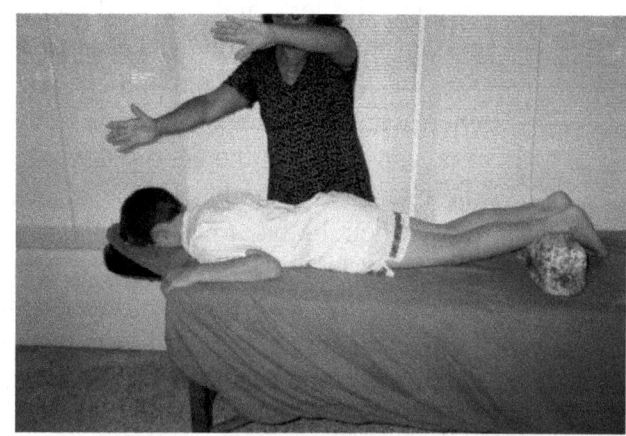

The Cocoon

The Spinal Zigzag

I use this technique on clients whom I know will be driving right after a healing session. Some clients are so relaxed during a Reiki treatment that they have fallen asleep. The last thing I want to see is the client behind the wheel of a car! For those clients who must drive home immediately following the session, I use this technique: Place the index and middle finger of either hand on the OUTSIDE of the client's spine. You will at NO time touch the client's spine. You can cause damage to the client should you press on their spine.

With your two fingers on the outside of the spine, you will make a zigzag movement with your fingers starting at the top of the spine and moving down to the bottom of the spine. Lift your fingers up off the body, return them to the top of the spine and repeat the zigzag motion down the spine for a total of three repetitions. When finished, I touch the client's shoulder (to signify the end of the session) and say Thank-You.

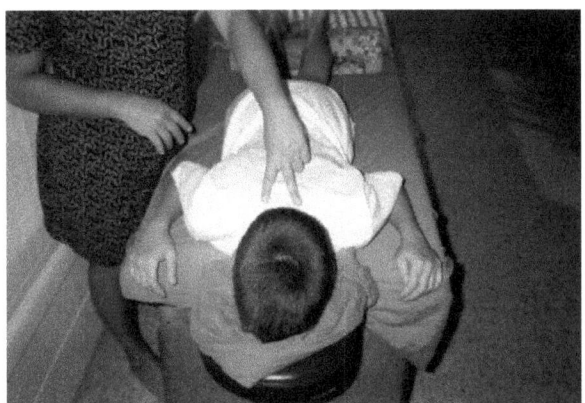

Day Two

Chapter Nine

Introduction to Tuning Forks

Welcome to the exciting world of sound therapy. As sound waves pass through the body, they elicit responses within the body's systems. These systems in turn react to the sound waves and vibrations and respond by restoring itself to a healthier and more harmonic base.

Each tuning fork is 'tuned' to a specific vibratory rate, or Hertz (cycles per second). The faster a tuning fork vibrates, the higher the pitch; the slower a tuning fork vibrates, the lower the pitch.

On the piano, for instance, the Middle C vibrates at 512 HZ (512 cycles per second). This vibration is often associated with the root chakra of an individual. It can help to ground a person and balance problems in the feet, knees and legs. On an emotional level, using the "C" tuning fork can help an individual deal with feelings of anger, impulsiveness, insecurity, fear and lack of trust.

Each tuning fork in the basic 8-piece set correlates to its own chakra, color, and vibration. Tuning forks can be used as a meditative practice, balancing each of the chakras and harmonizing the aura. Tuning forks can also be used to enhance the nutrition of food and water, as well as, to remove negative and stagnant energy in the room.

For acupuncturists and reflexologists, vibrating tuning forks can be used in place of needles on the reflex and acupuncture points of the body. While humans can benefit from a sound therapy session, pets and plants can also reap rewards from a tuning fork session. Pets often imitate and mirror many of the problems that their owners are experiencing and may benefit from a tuning fork session in much the same way as their owners.

When using tuning forks, know that sound is measured in movement or vibrations. This movement is referred to as Hertz or Hz for short. The number listed on each of the tuning forks is in Hz and correlates to the rate of vibrations per second that the tuning fork is associated with. The lower the number listed on the tuning fork, the slower the vibrations per second.

When the tuning fork is being used to correspond to the Middle C on the piano, the tines of the tuning fork are said to be vibrating at a frequency of 256 HZ (that's 256 vibrations per second). Likewise, a tuning fork listed as 512 HZ will vibrate at 512 vibrations per second—two times the frequency of the tuning fork).

Vibratory sounds can alter blood pressure, pulse rate, and breathing. It can also release muscle tension, regulate skin temperature and release pain, stress and tension. Harmonics is what enables you to hear a sound and recognize what instrument played it. It allows you to tell the difference between a C note being played on a piano and a C note being played on a flute.

It was the French physician, Alfred Tomatis, M.D. who studied the healing effects of sound and music on his patients. Often noted for using music on his patients, he was lovingly referred to as Dr. Mozart.

In his studies he believed that high frequency sounds (those that fall in the range of 3,000 to 8,000 HZ.) resonate in the brain and affect cognitive functions such as thinking, memory, and spatial perception.

These frequencies can also bring on immediate headaches and extreme disequilibrium. For others, frequencies in this range can be very stimulating activating the brain and increasing attentiveness. It is would be like a sonic Vitamin C.

He also discovered that middle frequencies, those that fall in the range of 750 to 3,000 HZ, tend to stimulate the heart, lungs and the emotions. Low frequencies, those that fall in the range of 125 to 750 HZ, can create stress, muscle contractions and pain. Low drone sounds tend to make us groggy while low fast rhythms make us fidgety and unable to concentrate.

Don Campbell, author of The Mozart Effect, found that ten minutes of drumming everyday releases tensions, resets the mind and body's inner clock, and serves as both a stimulant and sedative. This is because our bodies tend to match and adjust to the sounds, pace, pulse and rhythms that we hear. This is called entrainment, becoming 'in step' or 'in sync' with music.

History of the Tuning Fork

In 583 B.C., the Greek philosopher, Pythagoras, made a device called the monochord and set the pitch to 256Hz. The Greeks and Egyptians used the monochord to make intricate mathematical calculations.

In 1553 in Padua, Italy, H. Capivacci, a physician, noticed that this knowledge of sound being perceived through the skin might be used as a diagnostic tool for differentiating between hearing disorders located in the middle ear or in the acoustic nerve.

In 1711 in England, Royal trumpeter and lutenist, John Shore, created the first tuning fork. At the time, he lovingly and jokingly called it a pitch fork. It was made of steel and had a pitch of A423.5

In the 1960s the Swiss scientist Hans Jenny, discovered that low frequency sounds produced simple geometric shapes and as the sound frequency increased, the shapes became more complex. He also found that the sound 'OH' produced a perfect circle and that the sound 'OM' produced a pattern similar to that of the ancient Indian mandala for 'OM'.

In the late 1970s, a professional jazz musician Fabien Maman joined with the senior researcher at the National Centre for Scientific Research in Paris, Helene Grimal to study the effects of sound on normal and malignant cells. The pair used all types of sound making instruments including flutes, drums, gongs, and more.

They discovered that at 30-40 decibels, the sound always produced changes in the cells and the higher up the musical scale they went, the frequency would travel outward from the center of the cell to its outer membrane. The most amazing results happened when the human voice was used.

In an experiment on female volunteers with breast cancer, women were taught to tone the whole scale using a violin to keep a base note for 21 minutes at a time. They spent 3 ½ hours a day for one month. One woman's tumor disappeared completely.4

On the cellular level, Fabien Maman found that the note 'C' made them longer, 'D' produced a variety of colors, 'E' made them spherical, 'F' make them round, balanced and vibrant colors of magenta and turquoise, and 'A' (440Hz) changed the color of their energy field from red to pink. He also said that 'F' was the fundamental sound of the singer and thus helpful for the physical body through its harmonizing and regenerating effect at the cellular level.5

The Japanese scientist, Masaru Emoto, discovered that music affected water and that different types of music affected it differently. While he found that Classical music, folk music, and mantras produced beautiful crystals and colors, Heavy Metal music produced patterns that appeared exploded and shattered.

With our body made up of 80% water, Emoto's work demonstrates the importance of how our body is influenced by the sounds around us and by the information stored in the water that we drink.

Sound therapist Jonathan Goldman in his book *Healing Sounds* states that frequency plus Intention equals Healing. Barbara Hero and the International Lambdoma Research Institute in Kennebunk, Maine, discovered that by passing sound waves through each organ of the body that they were able to calculate the optimal frequency for each of the organs using mathematical formulas based on the speed of sound.

How to Activate your Tuning Fork

To strike your tuning fork correctly, you will need to hold the fork at the "foot" and strike the fork against the rubber surface with a firm "karate chop" motion. If you prefer a louder sound from the tuning fork, you can hit the fork against a hard surface, or against another tuning fork. Care should be taken when doing this since you run the risk of chipping or denting your tuning forks and losing the tone.

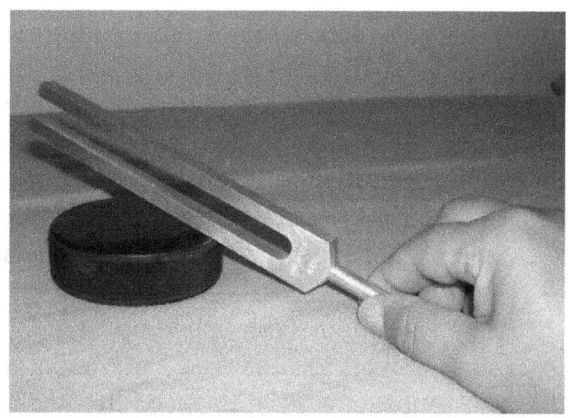

Precautions

Until further studies are done in using tuning forks, I would NOT use tuning forks on the following groups of people:

- Those with Pacemakers (stay away from the heart area)
- metal implants (this is for steel only as this material reverberates with vibrations-other materials are fine), metal pins or other metal bindings (only steel pins and bindings-all other material is fine)
- Pregnant Women (only in the abdominal area).
- Stay away from areas with stints and inserted tubes as they may dislodge.

How to Hold your Tuning Forks

The Correct Way to Hold your Tuning Fork

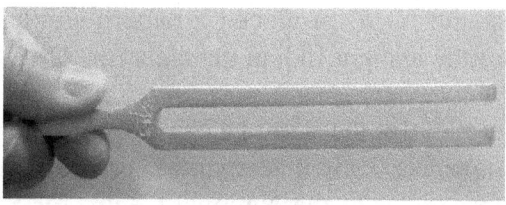

Do Hold Fork at End of Handle.

Keep wrist loose.

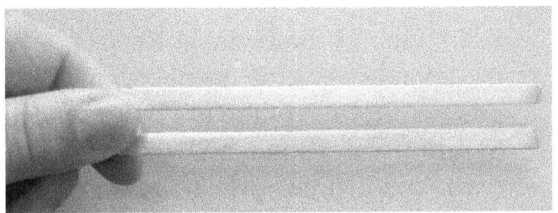

Do <u>not</u> grab the tuning fork close to the tines.

It may take some time to feel comfortable holding and activating your tuning forks. Do not become discouraged. With practice you will become confident in using them. You may wish to try using the unweighted tuning forks first before moving on to the weighted tuning forks. Unweighted tuning forks are much lighter and easier to hold for long periods of time.

Instructions for Toning the Tuning Fork

1. Use the Tuning Fork Activator

2. Use a Rubber Mallet

3. Tap the fork on your leg muscle

4. Tap the fork on the palm of your hand

5. Gently tap two (or more) forks together.

(Please note that tapping two forks together may cause them to chip or dent, and then they will lose their pitch and tone.)

Chapter Ten

The Genesis Tuning Fork

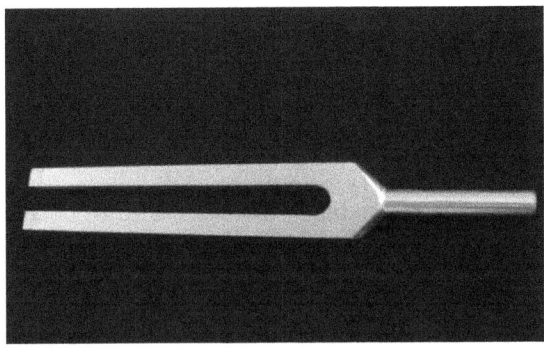

The Genesis Tuning Fork – 513 Hertz

The Genesis tuning fork can be purchased alone or as part of the Kabbalah set of tuning forks. This fork can be used alone, or combined with other tuning forks in your basic beginner set. Some practitioners have stated that when they use the Genesis and Gabriel tuning forks together they can repair damaged portions of DNA. These same practitioners also claim to use the Genesis fork with the Shekinah fork to destroy cancer cells. I make no judgment to these claims as I have yet to complete my research on this topic.

There is also the claim that the Genesis fork can move bones and joints back into place when they are out of alignment. The claims go further and add that the Genesis tuning fork will repair and rebuild muscle and tissue.

Again, I have no proof of any of this-but wouldn't that be wonderful? I would love to see actual documentation on these claims and would insist on doing so before I can spread such unsubstantiated claims.

The Genesis tuning fork is considered the 12th frequency and it is associated with the Archangel Michael.

Literally speaking, the word Genesis means 'beginning.' As the first book in the bible, it represents the beginning of creation. A broader translation of the word Genesis is, 'the beginning of something and how it came into being."

Scientifically speaking, Genesis (as in Biogenesis-the beginning of life) means a field of study. From chaos comes form. By using the Genesis tuning fork, we will create (or recreate) form.

The Symbols

In Vibrational Reiki™ we will incorporate several symbols in the healing process. In Level One we will use the **Infinity Symbol**, the **Rama** and the **Kriya**. In Level Two and Three, we will learn even more symbols to use in the process of healing. We will first begin with the Infinity Symbol

The Infinity Symbol

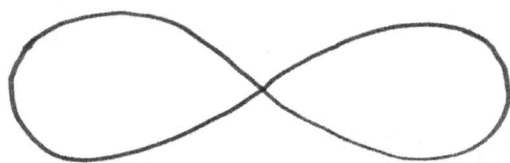

The symbol drawn above is called the **Infinity Symbol**

In Latin, the word '*infinity*' comes from the word '*infinita*' which means 'unboundedness.' But the concept of infinity isn't just one thing. The word, '*infinity*' refers to a variety of distinct concepts and ideas. Generally, all these concepts and ideas have one common thread-no end.

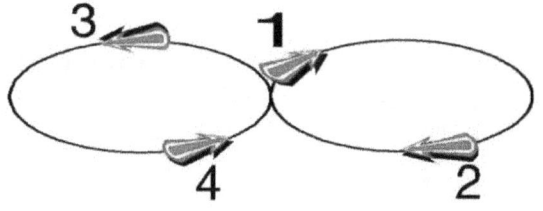

To draw the Infinity Symbol, start in the middle and flow upward to the right. Continue downward and to the left meeting in the middle where I started. Continue by swooping upward and to the left, downward and to the right until meeting in the middle once again. When drawing the Infinity Symbol, I draw three complete symbols-one over top of the other.

Another way to draw the Infinity Symbol is shown below:

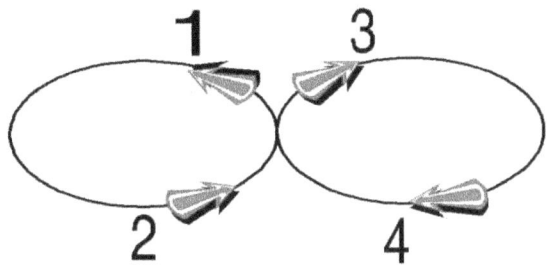

In Mathematics, "infinity is used as both a number and a measure. As a number, "infinity" is the largest possible number. It is the Absolute Infinite.

John Wallis has been credited for introducing the infinity symbol in 1655. As a measure, "infinity" is the furthest possible distance.

In philosophy, the word "infinity" is used to convey both time and space. It is explored as the Absolute, God and the Ultimate. It is boundless. It is the origin of all that is. It is also the sense of being without limits or existing without constraints.

When referring to time, the infinity symbol is often seen as the snake biting its own tail (which is what create the circle). It signifies the balance of the upper and lower natures. The infinity symbol is also seen as an empty circle. It is endless-it symbolizes eternity.

Some people have claimed that the infinity symbol comes from the Latin word *lemniscuses*, meaning "ribbon." This is why you may have heard the infinity symbol sometimes referred to as the lemniscates. The infinity symbol has even been found in Tibetan rock carvings.

In the Rider-Waite tarot card deck, the infinity symbol is often associated with the magician's card where the Magician is portrayed with an infinity symbol over his head. In the card deck, the symbol is used to represent the balance of forces.

The infinity symbol is a sacred geometric shape which represents the delicate balance in life. It is the oneness of all that is. In marriage and relationships, the two circles represent two rings coming together symbolizing both partners coming together as one. When in balance, the marriage allows each to be individuals and yet together they are one. When out of balance, then the harmony of the marriage or relationship is at stake.

The infinity symbol can bring balance back into the human body. When illness or disease finds its way into the body, it throws off the balance of the body. The symbol will help bring the body back into balance. Being infinite-the infinity symbol will also bring in infinite love, infinite joy, infinite potential, infinite possibilities, etc.

It has been said that, at the 10th dimension; the infinity symbol will demonstrate the hermetic principle of "as above, so below." This alone will open up great opportunities for both the healer and the client.

To Draw the Infinity Symbol over Client

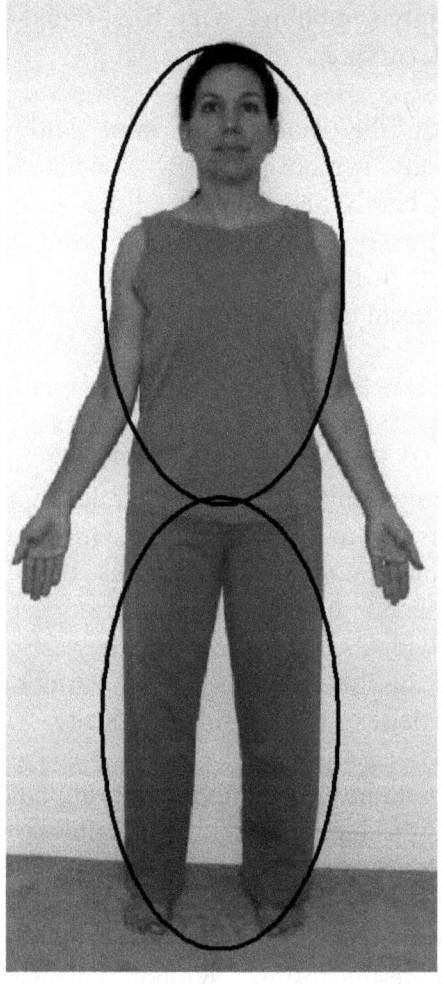

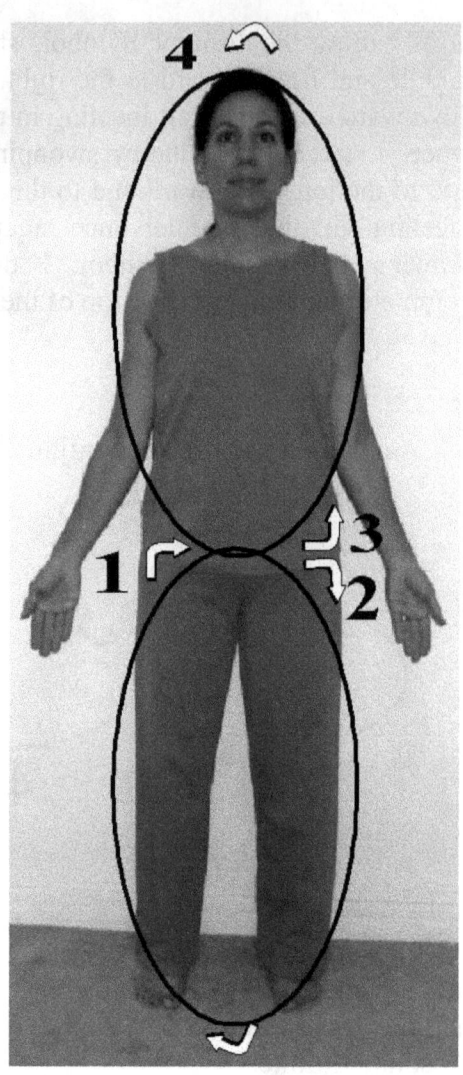

Start at the center of your client's sacral chakra (just below the navel). You will be standing to the right of your client. Sweep upward and to the right, down the left side of your client's body, underneath the client's feet, up the right side of the body to the center. Then sweep upward and to the left, over the client's head and down the right side of your client's body to meet at the center. Repeat for a total of three sweeps.

Another option is to start at the center of your client's sacral chakra and sweep upward and to the left over the client's head and down the right side of your client's body, back to the center. Then sweep downward and to the right down the left side of your client's body to below their feet and up the right side to meet at the center. Repeat for a total of three sweeps.

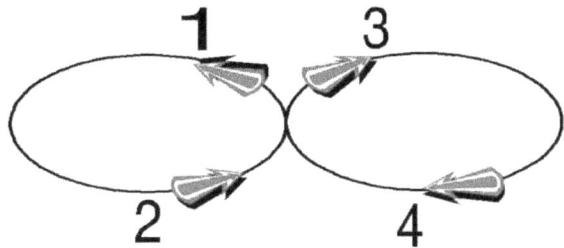

Instead of a full body sweep, you can do a smaller version. Start at the center of your client's heart chakra. Sweep upward and to the right down to the root chakra (below the pubic bone) and up the right side of the body to the center. Then sweep upward and to the left, over the client's head and down the right side of your client's body to meet at the center. Repeat for a total of three sweeps.

Vertical

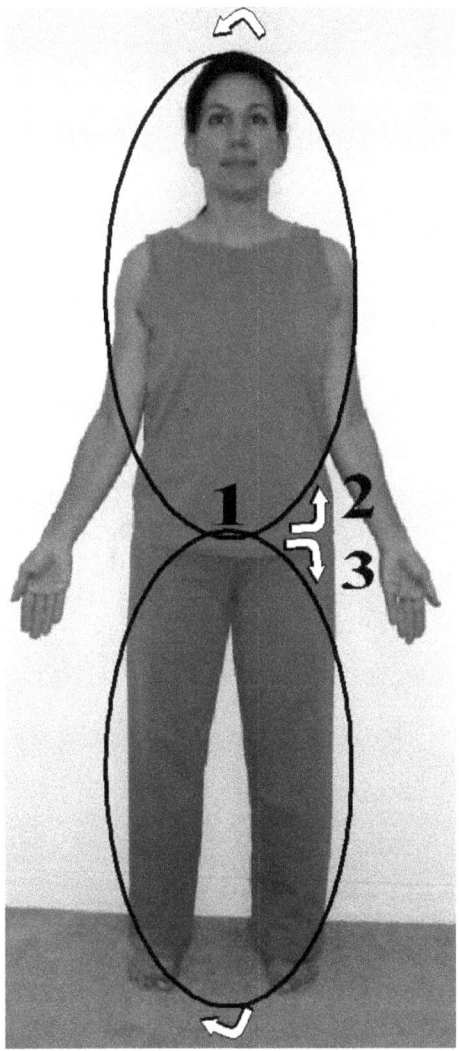

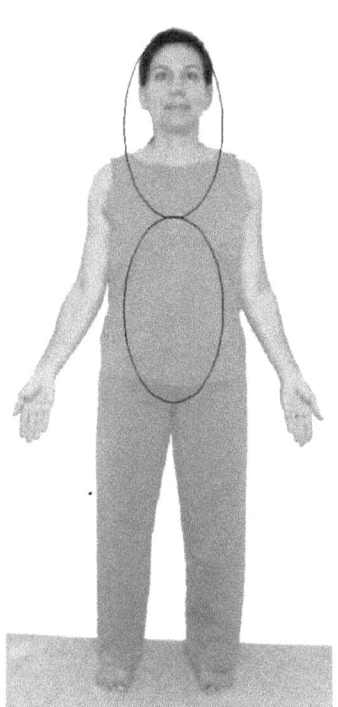

You can also choose to use the infinity symbol in a horizontal or vertical position like in the photographs below:

Horizontal   **Vertical**

Root Chakra

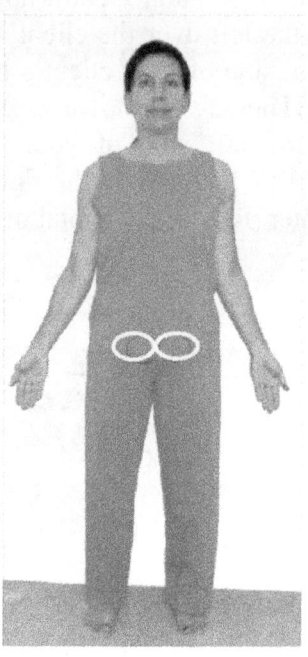

Sacral Chakra

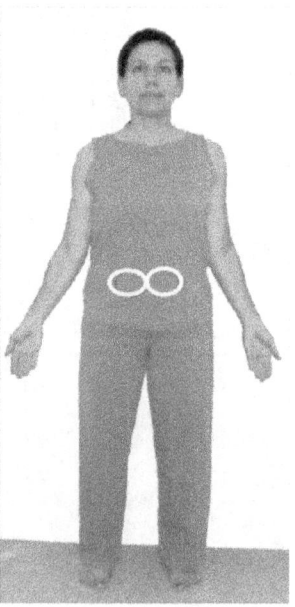

Solar Plexus Chakra

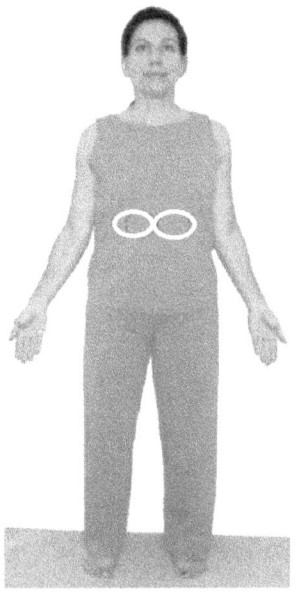

Throat Chakra

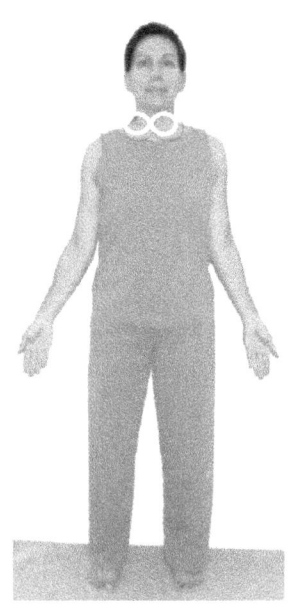

Heart Chakra

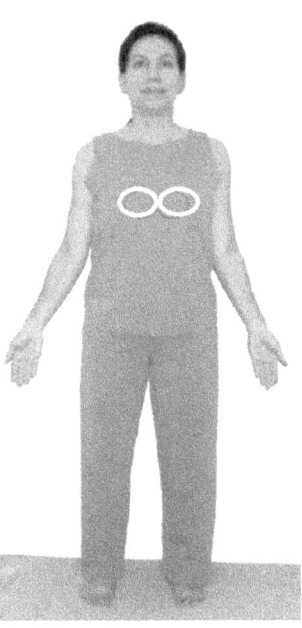

Brow Chakra

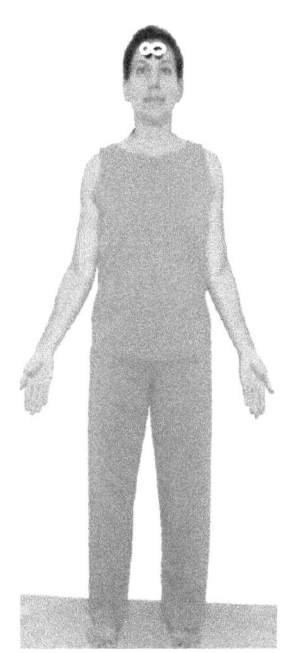

Crown Chakra

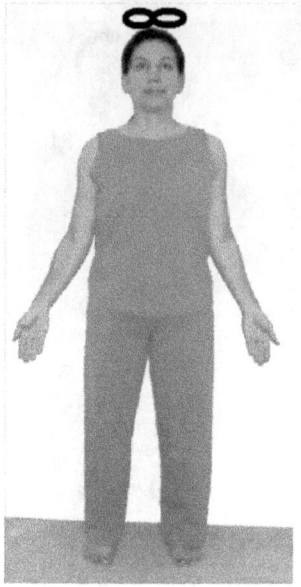

The Tuning Fork Session using the Infinity Symbol for the Reclining Position

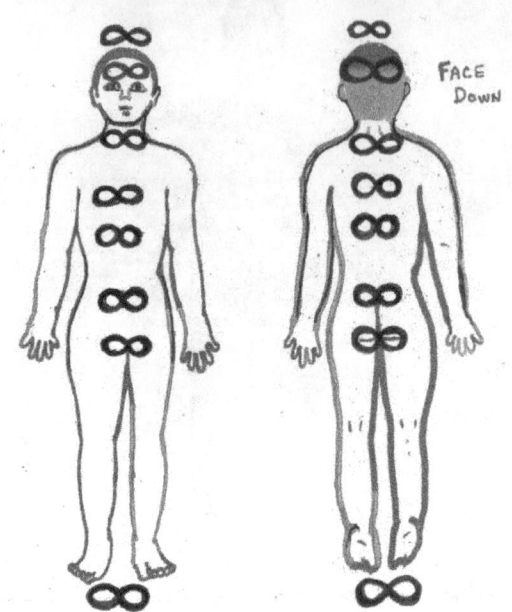

Earth Chakra

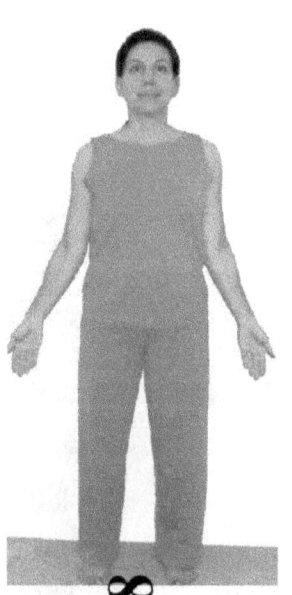

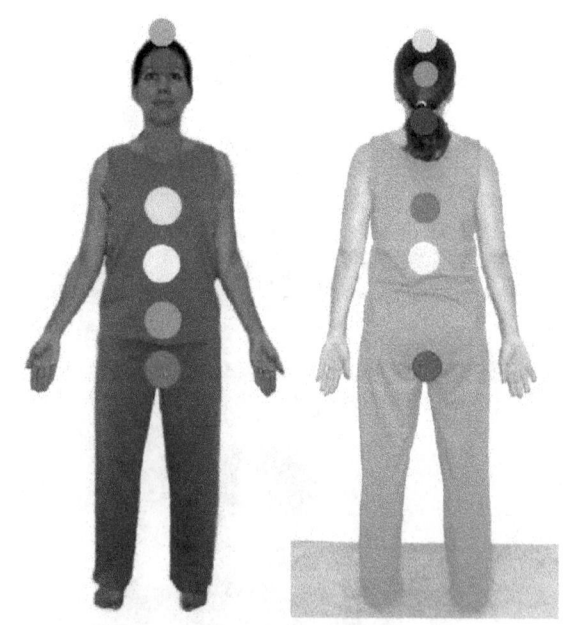

Using the Infinity Symbol on yourself

You can draw the Infinity symbol on yourself and others in a seated position as follows:

- First take a deep breath in and strike the Genesis tuning fork.
- Draw the Infinity symbol over your root chakra area three times. Shake the tuning fork off, activate it again, and repeat for a total of three repetitions.

Go slowly and count to 20 while making one symbol (or allow yourself whatever time you need). Shake off the fork. Repeat two more times, for a total of three times.

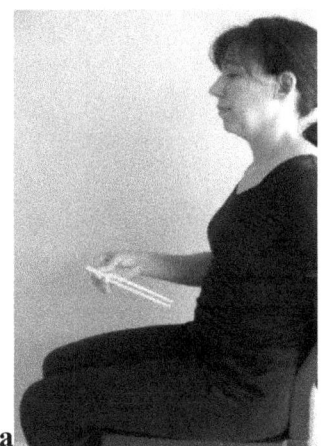
Sacral Chakra

Solar Plexus

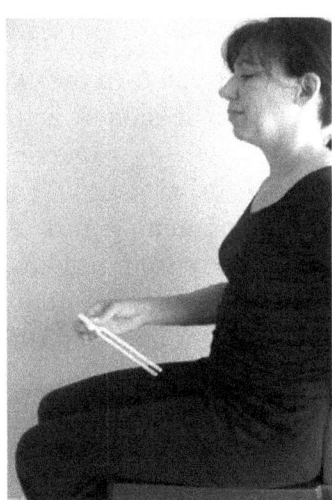
Root Chakra

Heart Chakra

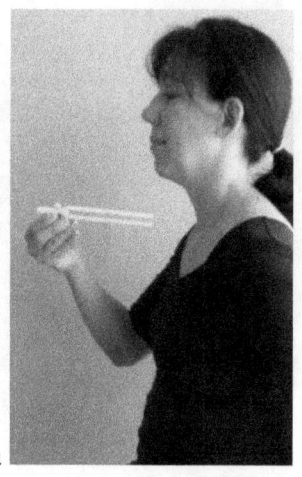
Throat Chakra

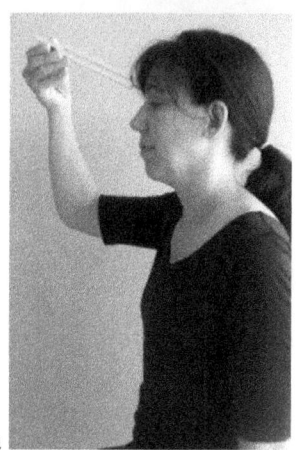
Brow Chakra

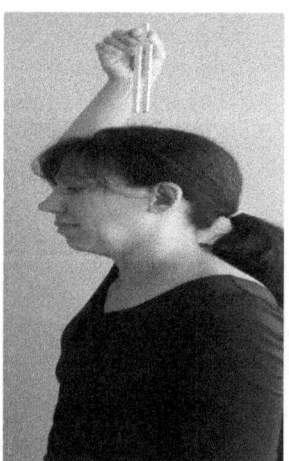
Crown Chakra

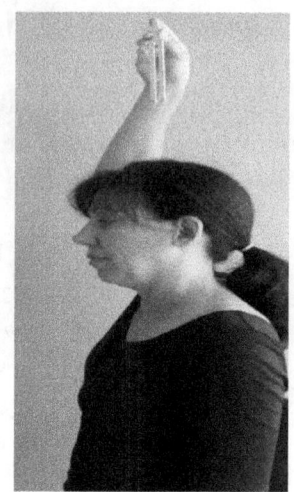
Soul Star

Closing Techniques:

When finished, perform a closing technique:

1. Activate the Genesis fork and draw one Infinity Symbol right in front of you.

2. If you own the OM tuning fork, you may end your session by activating that tuning fork.

3. Strike your OM tuning fork and run the vibrating tuning fork down the right side of your body from head to toe and back up again. Shake the tuning fork off. Strike your OM tuning fork a second time and run the vibrating tuning fork down the middle of your body from head to toe. Shake your tuning fork off. Strike your OM tuning fork for the third time and run the vibrating tuning fork down the left side of your body from head to toe. Shake the fork off.

4. You may also choose to sit quietly and allow your body to absorb the energy that you have just received.

Using the Symbol on seated partner

Activate your tuning fork and draw the infinity symbol three times on the root chakra. Shake off the tuning fork and activate it again. Repeat the process for a total of three repetitions. When finished, move on to the next chakra.

#1 Root Chakra

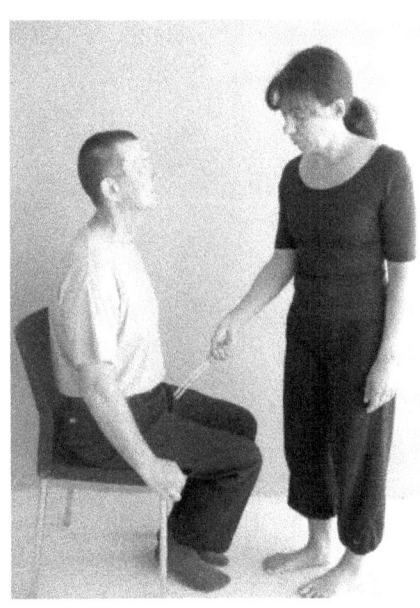

#2 Sacral Chakra

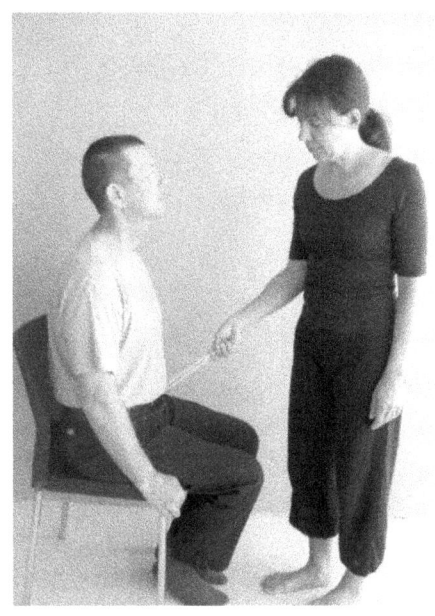

#3. Solar Plexus Chakra

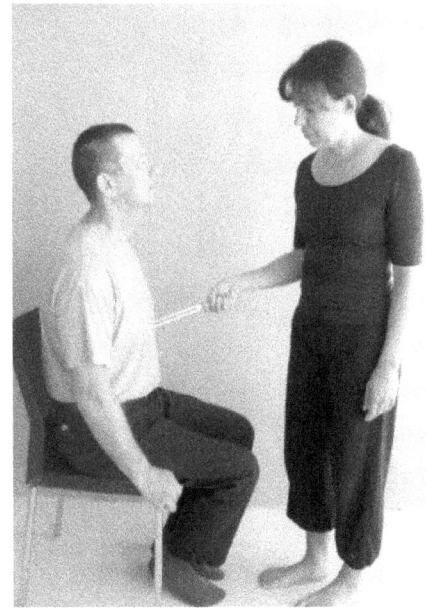

#4 Heart Chakra

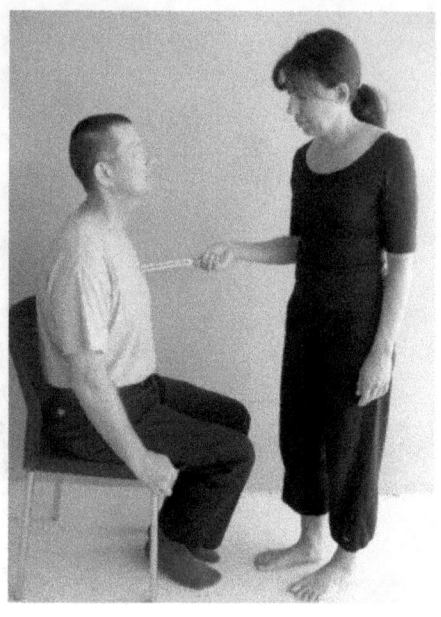

#6 Brow Chakra

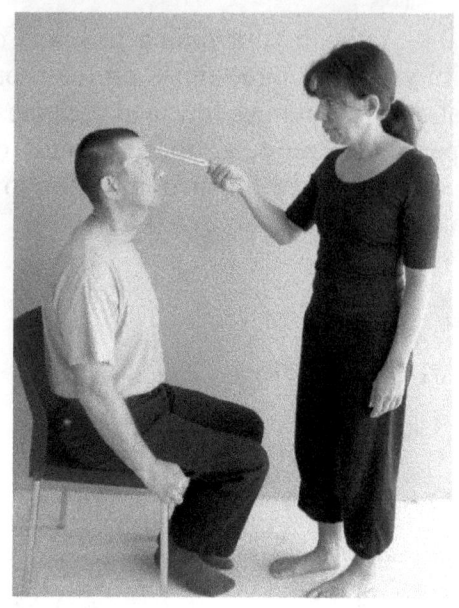

#5 Throat Chakra

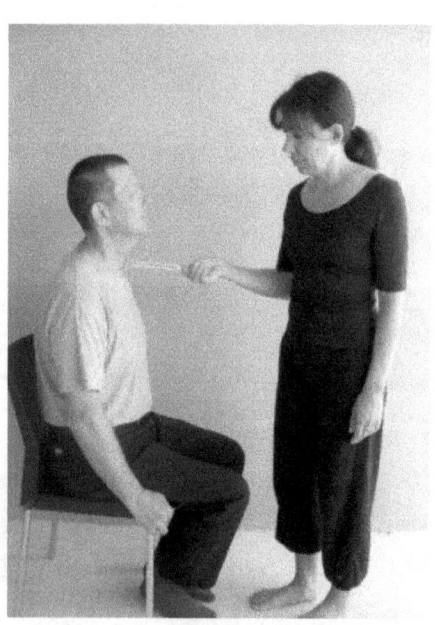

#7 Crown Chakra

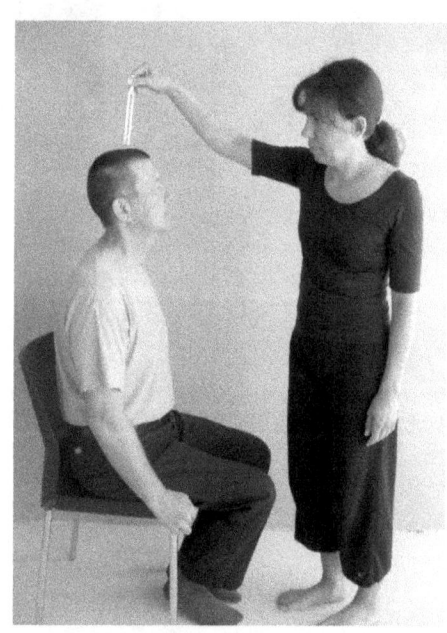

Closing Techniques:

When finished, I will perform a closing technique as follows:

1. Activate the Genesis fork and sweep the vibrating tuning fork from above your client's head down their body to the floor (counting 10 seconds) and back up again (counting 10 seconds). Shake it off and repeat the process going down the right side of your client and back up again. Shake it off and repeat going down the front of your client and back up again. Shake it off and repeat going down the left side of your client and back up again.
2. Tap your client on their shoulder when you are finished and say, "Thank You." This will signal to your client that you have finished the session.

Chapter Eleven

Additional Symbols

RAMA

According to Vincent Amador of Karuna Ki, the original symbol *RAMA*, pronounced "ra ma," was channeled by Kellie-ray Marine. Translated, the word RAMA means "abiding joy" and is interchangeable with Ram, or God.

RAMA has many uses, but the most popular use is that of grounding. This is especially helpful when you are doing energy work on your client. Drawing this symbol over your client will help to ground them after each of your sessions. This is very, very important.

When used on the hips and legs of your client, the RAMA symbol can be used to open and heal the lower chakras in addition to grounding. When this symbol is used on the total body of your client, RAMA can clear away any blockages in the body and ground the person.

You may also draw the RAMA symbol over the whole body to connect the lower chakras with the upper chakras to bring harmony, wholeness and oneness into the body. This is especially helpful for people who live too much in their heads, or for others who have too many basic fears in life. If you have a client who is stuck on over indulgences (obesity, sex, alcohol, etc.) or a client who is stuck in lack or need, this is the perfect symbol to use on them.

RAMA can also be used to manifest material goals. I believe that this happens because of the ability of this symbol to ground you. Once you become grounded, you increase focus. I believe that it is this ability to gain focus that helps you to manifest in the present. But that is my opinion.

Drawing the RAMA symbol over the entire body of your client

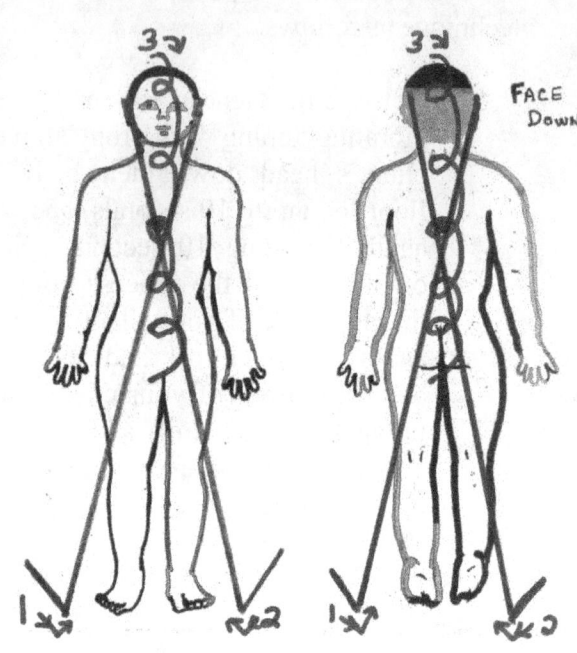

The way you would draw this symbol is to start at the foot of your client and begin at the right foot of the client and pass the vibrating tuning fork up to their left shoulder. Then take the vibrating tuning fork and run it from the left foot of the client up to their right shoulder. Now take the still vibrating tuning and start at their crown chakra (top of their head), and start looping the chakras downward to the space between their feet. Shake off the tuning fork when finished.

NOTE: The Third loop intersects the two check marks at client's Heart Chakra.

Alternative RAMA

RAMA of the Chakras

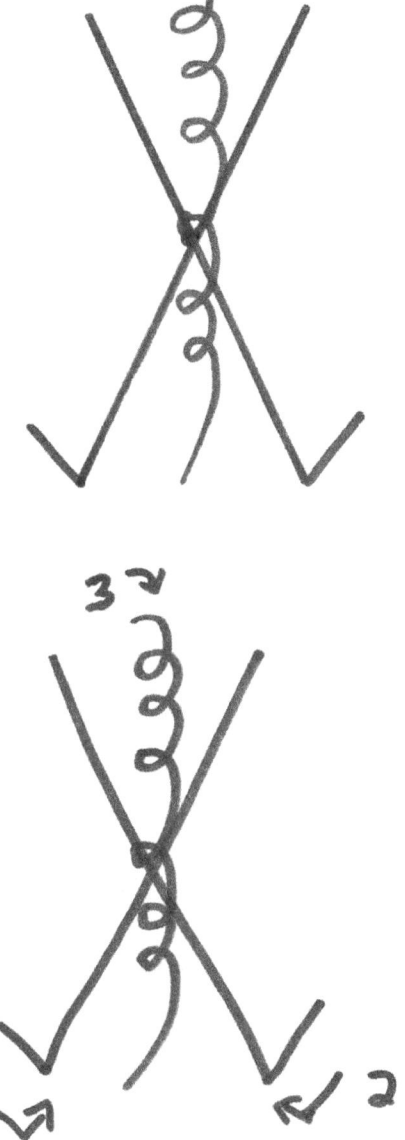

If you look at the RAMA symbol drawn above and the RAMA Symbol drawn previously, you will see one major difference. The loops that are drawn in the middle of the two check marks have an additional loop added to it.

The way you would draw this symbol is to start at the left foot of the client and pass the vibrating tuning fork up to their left shoulder. The two check marks would intersect at the client's Solar Plexus Chakra.

Then take the vibrating tuning fork and run it from the right foot of the client up to their right shoulder. Now take the still vibrating tuning and start at their crown chakra (top of their head), and start looping the chakras downward to the space between their feet.

Shake off the tuning fork when finished.

NOTE: The Fourth loop intersects the two check marks.

Assignment: Practice drawing the symbol on both the front and back of your client.

Drawing the Alternative RAMA over your client

KRIYA

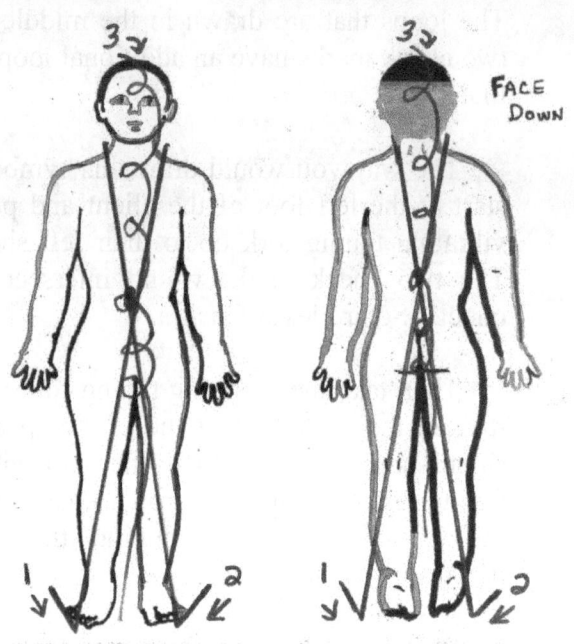

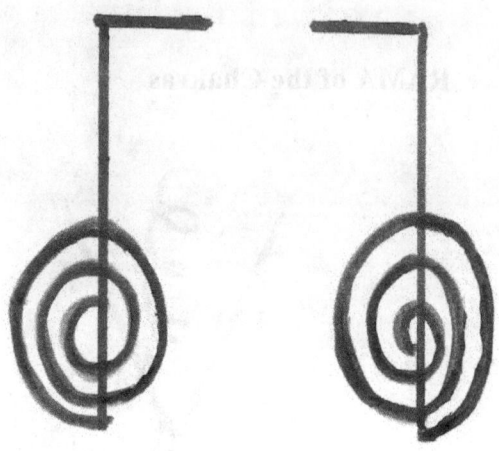

Start with your client face up and with you standing at their feet. Begin drawing the symbol at the right foot of the client and pass the vibrating tuning fork up to their left shoulder and then from the left foot to the right shoulder.. The two check marks would intersect at the client's Solar Plexus Chakra.

Then take the vibrating tuning fork and run it from the right foot of the client up to their right shoulder. Now take the still vibrating tuning and start at their crown chakra (top of their head), and start looping the chakras downward to the space between their feet. Shake off the tuning fork when finished.

NOTE: The Fourth loop intersects the two check marks.

KRIYA is a symbol that was channeled by Pat Miller. Pronounced, 'Kree yah,' this symbol represents balance. The symbol is a mirror image of each other. Some people call this symbol the double Cho-Ku-Rei.

This symbol is an **action** symbol that can either <u>bring in</u> energy, or <u>release</u> energy. Use your intention when drawing this symbol. This symbol is also very grounding and when drawn over the person starting at the hips with the spirals at their feet.

You can use this symbol to close the client after a healing session. Like the RAMA, this symbol can also be used to bring about material manifestation as this symbol can transform our ideas and thoughts into action and help you to focus on your priorities.

To draw the symbol KRIYA

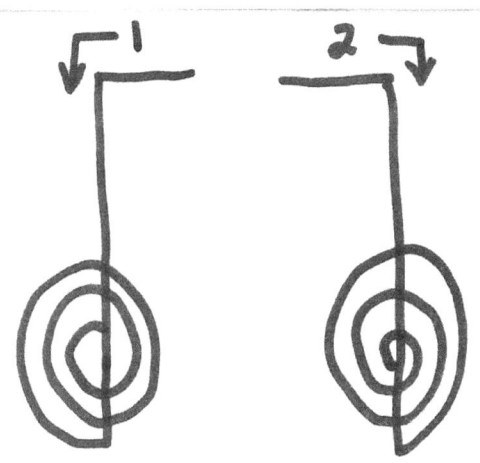

To draw the symbol KRIYA, you will first activate your tuning fork and start about one hand width below your client's navel and draw the first line out to the right hip of your client (who is lying face up on the massage table). You will follow that line down your client's leg to their feet where you will draw the spirals moving in a clockwise fashion.

You will draw the symbol again this time beginning at the point one hand width below your client's navel and draw the line out to your client's left hip and down their leg making spirals moving in a counterclockwise fashion at their feet. Shake of the tuning fork and repeat this process for a total of three repetitions.

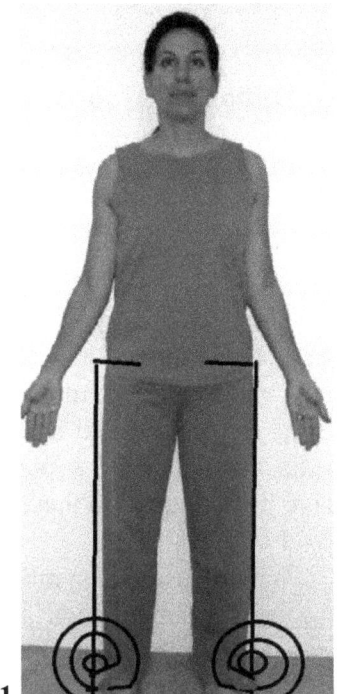

Option #1

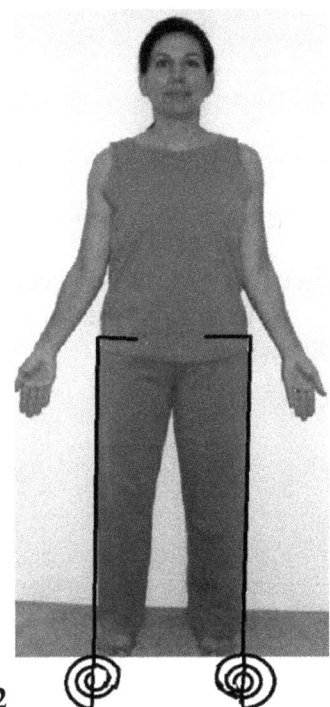

Option #2

Option #1-At the Feet

Option #2-Below the Feet

The KRIYA symbol can be drawn using two exact tuning forks at the same time. You may choose to just draw the KRIYA symbol using just your Reiki and not using the tuning forks at all. This is perfectly alright as you have been attuned to these symbols.

When I use this symbol in Reiki sessions, I use both of my hands at the same time and draw this symbol over the client. As I am doing this, I am repeating the symbol's name each time I draw it (Three times).

Note: To take energy out, you will continue to do the spirals and out and away from the client's body and direct it to the floor where it can be transmuted into love. Use your intention.

Assignment: Practice drawing the KRIYA symbol on the front and back of your client.

Body Scanning

Using the tuning fork in Body Scanning

Activate the tuning fork and place it 1"-2" above the body and starting from above the crown chakra run it down the front of the client to below their feet. Activate it again and run from the below the feet up to the top of their crown chakra.

Watch the fork very carefully for any shaking, twisting, dipping or other movements that are not fluid. This would signify an area in need of work. Listen for any changes in pitch or tone as this too would be an area in need.

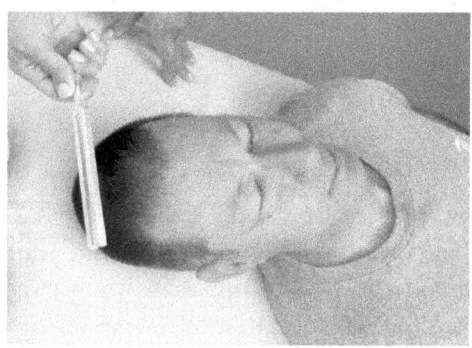

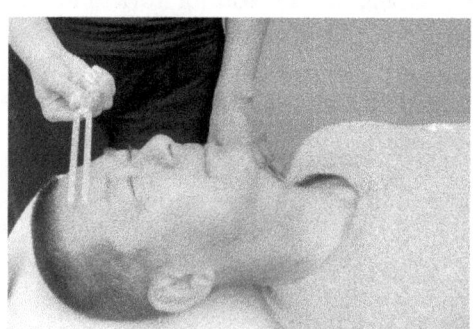

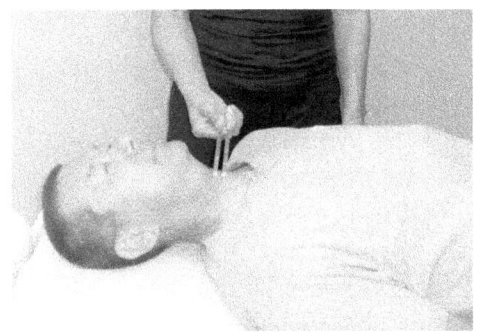

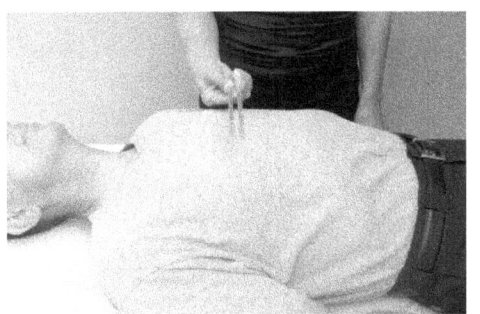
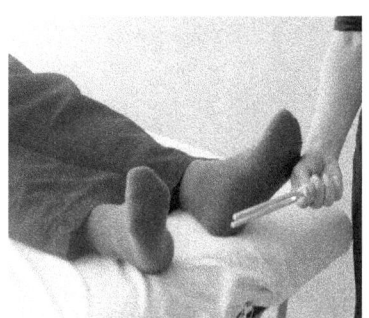

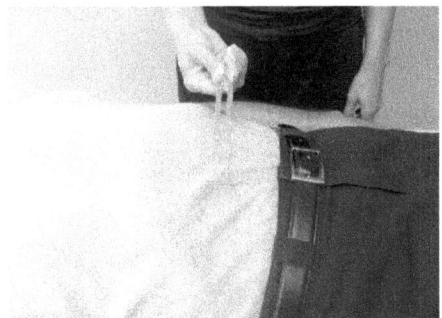

After you have done the body scan on the chakras, be sure to include the legs and arms, one at a time.

If you find something that needs work, stop and place the vibrating tip of the tuning fork directly only the area in need. Keep the fork in place for 20-30 seconds and repeat for a total of three repetitions. Then scan the area again to see if you made a change. If the area needs more work, then continue to work on it until it is finished, and the scan comes back clear.

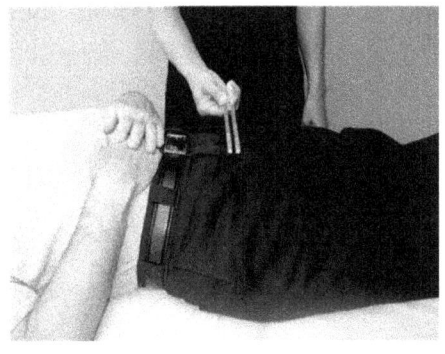

Use the tuning fork in the aura

Just like you did the scan with your hands in the layers of the aura, you can activate the tuning fork and lower it through the layers of the aura over every one of the chakras, including the knees and ankles.

When working on the crown chakra and the feet, you go through the layers horizontally instead of vertically.

As you go through the layers, watch the vibrating tuning fork very carefully for any shaking, twisting, dipping or other movements that are not fluid. This would signify an area in need of work. Listen for any changes in pitch or tone as this too would be an area in need.

If you find an area in need, stop and draw the infinity symbol in that area three times and then scan the area again. Continue this process until the area scans as clean.

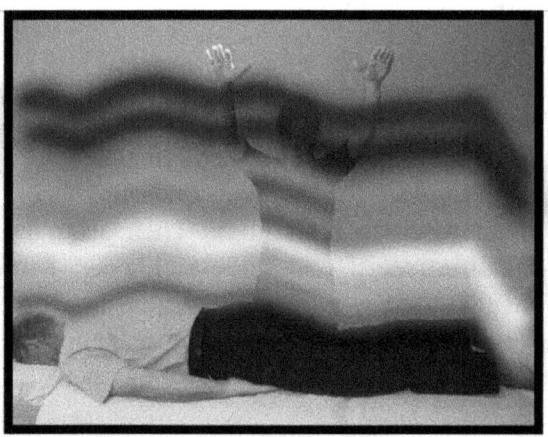

Using the Symbols on the table

The Vibrational Reiki™ Session

Just like the previous technique where we drew the Infinity symbol on someone sitting in a chair, we will now draw the symbol on someone lying down on a massage table. Begin with the root chakra and move up the sacral, solar plexus, heart, throat, brown, crown and soul star chakra. Finish with the earth chakra to give a grounding effect to the energy.

In the Vibrational Reiki™ healing session, we will proceed as follows:

- Have the client lay on a massage table, face up.
- Activate the Genesis tuning fork and do your body and aura scanning.
- With the activated Genesis tuning fork, make the Infinity Symbol starting at the client's root chakra. Draw the infinity symbol three times in one activation. Shake it off and activate the tuning fork again and repeat drawing the Infinity symbol on the root chakra for a total of three repetitions.
- When finished, activate the Genesis tuning fork and make the Infinity Symbol three times over the sacral chakra. Continue this process moving on to the solar plexus, heart, throat, brow, crown, the soul star chakra (located 10-12" above the head). Finish with the earth chakra (located 10-12" below the feet).
- Close session.
- When finished, tap the client on their shoulder and say, 'Thank-you.'

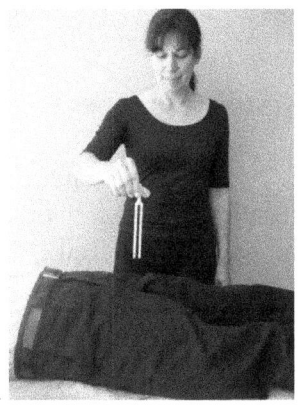
Root Chakra

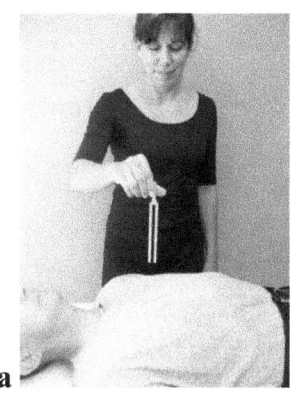
Heart Chakra

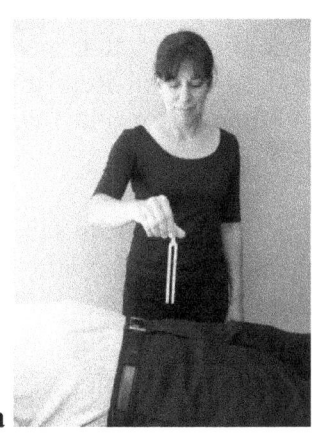
Sacral Chakra

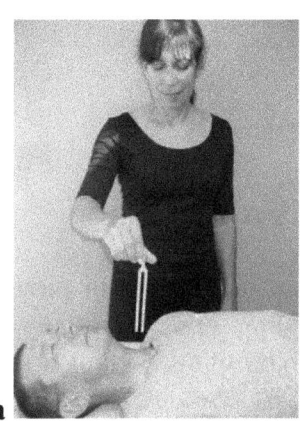
Throat Chakra

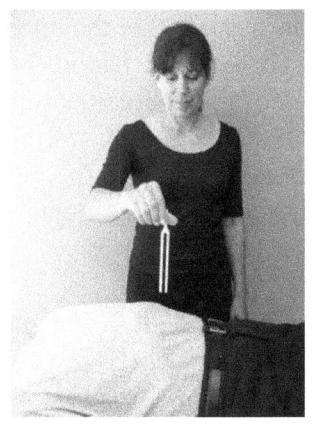
Solar Plexus

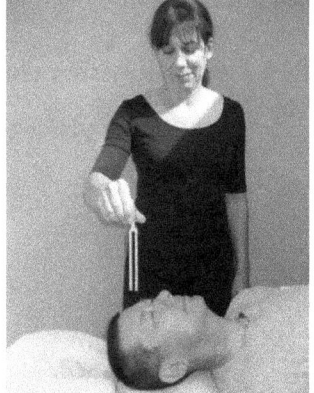
Brown Chakra

Crown Chakra

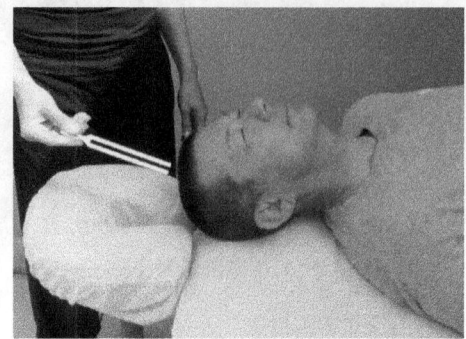

Assignment:

Have your partner lay on the massage table and practice drawing the Infinity Symbol on each of the chakras.

When finished with the front of the chakras, turn your client over and practice drawing the Infinity Symbol on each of the back chakras.

Finish with a closing of your choice.

Hygienic Concerns for the Practitioner

It is a general belief by many Vibrational Reiki™ practitioners and students that Vibrational Reiki™ is a hands-on healing technique. Well, yes and no. The human touch is a valuable and loving modality, but there are times when touching another person are impossible.

Vibrational Reiki™ can work not only on the physical body of a person but also in the auric field of that person also. It is highly advised that all Reiki practitioners adopt some common sense and hygienic practices to their healing sessions.

First, get into the habit of washing your hands before and after each treatment. This cleansing procedure will have a double benefit. In the field of energy, external forces can affect the energetic field.

Washing your hands before a session not only is proper hygiene, it also acts as a cleansing of the practitioners own energy field. This assures that the client will receive not only clean, washed hands, but hands that are also free of the energetic "junk" of the practitioners. This holds doubly true for washing hands after a treatment where the practitioner will not want to take on their clients' physical dis-ease nor their "junk" energy.

Secondly, change the sheets and wash them after each session. Some practitioners believe that because their clients are fully dressed for a session that they do not have to strip the sheets and wash them between clients.

This is both unpleasant and unsanitary. Would you want to lie on sheets that have been used by not one, but several people before you? Of course not, so why would you subject someone else to that. It is not only the physical body that I am concerned about but also the energetic body. Would you want to lie in someone else's left over energies? I know I sure wouldn't.

Be sure to wipe down your massage table, as well as the sheets after each session. A good disinfectant would be fine, or you can purchase a spray specifically formulated and designed for massage therapists by ordering online or visiting your local alternative health care store. Take the time necessary to supply your clients with a safe and healthy environment for their healing sessions.

Thirdly, if your client has any burns, open sores, blisters, cuts, etc. DO NOT put your hands on those areas of the body. You can work just as effectively and safely a few inches above the area in question.

In most states, expect a visit from a state health inspector who will ensure that proper procedures are followed. Every state requirement is different, but most follow the same general rules and regulations for their massage therapist as they do for Vibrational Reiki™ practitioners. Before setting up your practice, check with your own state on your local requirements to practice Vibrational Reiki™ in your area.

Legal issues

Whenever one person "lays" or "places" their hand on another person's body, a potential for harm exists. It is this concept that has many regulating bodies up in arms and with good reason. How can you regulate Reiki practitioners? How can you give Reiki practitioners one set of rules for all of them to follow? How can you insure that all Reiki practitioners are taught proper hygiene techniques? Well, because of this and other reasons, many states have taken it upon themselves to find a way to regulate the practice of Reiki.

Each Reiki practitioner comes into the field of Reiki energy work with their own set of values and healing arts. Some practitioners use only Reiki in their sessions while other practitioners use Reiki as an adjunct to other forms of healing. The client (the public at large) does not really know if what they are receiving is truly Reiki, or some sort of other treatment to which Reiki has been added. There are no true guidelines on this subject to date.

There is the issue of insurance. When you are involved with the public, there is a question of risk and the possibility of being sued. What if the person claims you caused them severe damage or falls off your massage table and breaks their hip? What if they sue you? Some practitioners believe that if they give their services away for free that they cannot be sued. I hate to burst your bubble, but yes, you can be sued. If you having something that can be taken away from you in a lawsuit (home, car, and other valuables), then you should sincerely consider carrying insurance on yourself.

Yes, there are companies out there who insure Reiki practitioners. If you are a massage therapist, or other licensed health care practitioner, then you probably are already carrying insurance on yourself, but you should check and be sure that Reiki will be covered under your current policy. Don't expect someone else to do this for you; this is your responsibility, so take care of it now!

Please, never manipulate (massage) your client without proper certifications, training, and licenses. If you are not experienced, you can cause great damage to your client. Leave massages to the licensed massage therapist.

Some states require that a Reiki practitioner must be a licensed massage therapist or a licensed and practicing medical doctor. To be sure of the requirements in your own particular state, you must call and ask your own licensing boards. Never assume because so and so down the street is practicing Reiki without a license that it is all right for you to do the same. It may not be. If you are caught practicing without a license you can be fined, or worse. So be sure to find out your legal standing first before you hang out your shingle.

But for using tuning forks, I can find no law governing this system of healing. But check with your own state first AND local licensing bureaus.

Put it All Together in a Healing Session

Now that you have been practicing a variety of methods and techniques, it is time to put what you have learned into a typical healing session.

First, you must understand that no two sessions are alike. But with this first level of training, I have found that the general protocols that work with one client, work for another. It is amazing. I have been giving tuning fork treatments for more than 20 years, and it has held true.

You can perform the tuning fork session as a stand-alone treatment. The tuning forks session can be done in the 30-60 minute routine. The tuning fork session can also be added as a service to your regular massage or bodywork session.

When added to a regular massage therapy session, the massage therapist may come across knots in muscles that they are unable to smooth out. For these tough areas, you can place the tip of the handle of a vibrating tuning fork directly onto the area of the body in need. Repeat the process for as many times as you feel will help the client. I use three repetitions a lot in my own practice, but when the client needs more, I give more.

The tuning forks can also be used before a session to help the client become relaxed and ready for a massage treatment. Many therapists have commented on how relaxed the clients become after using tuning forks in the session before giving their clients a massage.

Using the tuning forks to close a massage therapy session is also a nice finishing touch for those who value sound and vibration. I would ask the client first before assuming that they would like the use of tuning forks on them. Some people will not appreciate the use of tuning forks in their massage session, always ask for permission first. In fact, I always ask permission for no matter what additional therapy I want to use in the session. Leave it up to the client as to what they feel comfortable with at that moment in time. And be prepared; they might change their mind at their next session.

Note: A regular session should take at least one hour. Take your time while performing the passes. Remember, the slower you move the vibrating tuning fork, the more powerful it is.

Client In-take Form

If you don't have one already, one of the first things you should do as a tuning fork healing practitioner, is to create your own client in-take form. This form should provide you with information on a specific client, and your clientele in general. This is also your future mailing list. Through this form, you learn about the demographics of where you practice.

You will also learn about whom comes to you for healing sessions i.e.: male vs. female, average age of clientele, referrals, general complaints of clients, etc. With this knowledge, you will be able to design your ads, brochures, business cards, etc. to target your market groups.

Always make notes of any complaints the client may make, and encourage your clients to let you in on what they are experiencing. Make notes if certain sounds bother them, or how certain "areas" of their body are responding to the tuning fork sessions, etc. Be sure to date your information and do a follow up with the client to see what, if any, progress they are making. You should make your own client forms, or use a standard one that is available in many office supply houses.

On the next page is a sample of a client in-take form that you can use or make up and personalize one of your own.

Date_____

Client Name _____

Address _____

Telephone _____

E-Mail _____

Initial Complaint _____

Doctor _____

Person to Call in Case of Emergency
_____

Pregnant? _____

Any Heart Conditions? Pacemaker? Stents?
_____

If yes, please list:

_____

Any metal pins, bindings, or screws?
_____

If yes, what materials are they made of?
_____

If yes, where are they located?:

_____
_____
_____

List any pre-existing illnesses or ailments

_____
_____
_____

Do you currently have a Colonoscopy bag, catheter, tubing? If yes, where?

_____

Any blood clots, aneurisms, etc.?
If yes, where is it?

_____
_____

Can you lay on a massage table for a one hour treatment? _____

If no, why not?

_____

Protocol Followed

(In this space, write down your initial treatment protocols and your findings. You may also wish to add your client's feedback and your own intuition on what is occurring with your client. You may wish to make further suggestions, such as follow-up treatments, nutrition advice, emotional support, etc.)

_____
_____
_____
_____
_____

Additional Comments or Notes:

78

Protocols for Spot Treatment

NOTE: Be sure to do the hand position for BOTH the front and back chakras that are listed below.

Abdominal Pains—Chakra 1, 2, and 3

Acne—Chakra 1, 2, 3, and 4

Addictions—Chakra (All and Any)

Adenoid Problems—Chakra 5, 6, and 7

Adrenal—Chakra 1, 2, and 4

AIDS—Chakra 1, 2, 4, and 6

Allergies—Chakra 3, 4, and 5

Alzheimer's—Chakra 1, 2, 3, 4, and 6

Anemia—Chakra 1, 2, 3, and 4

Angina—Chakra 3, 4, 5, 6, and 7

Ankle Problems—Chakra 1, 2, 3, and 4

Anxiety—Chakra 1, 2, 3, and 4

Appendicitis—Chakra 1, 2

Arms Problems—Chakra 2, 4

Arteries—Chakra 1, 2, and 4

Arthritis—Chakra 1, 3, and 4

Asthma—Chakra 2, 3, and 4

Athlete's Foot—Chakra 1, 2, 3, and 4

Back Problems—All the Chakras

Bedwetting—Chakra 1, 2, and 3

Bladder Problems—Chakra 1, 2, and 3

Bleeding—Chakra 1, 4

Blood Problems—All the Chakras

Blood Pressure (High)—Chakra 3, 4

Blood Pressure (Low)—Chakra 1, 2, 3, and 4

Bone Problems—Chakra 1, 2, 3, 4, and 5

Bowel Problems—Chakra 1, 2, and 3

Brain Problems—Chakra 1, 4, 6, and 7

Breast Problems—Chakra 4

Bronchitis—Chakra 1, 2, and 4

Bursitis—Chakra 1, 3, 4, and 5

Cancer—Chakra 3, 4, and 5

Cervical Cancer—Chakra 1, 2, 4, 5, and 6

Cholesterol Problems—Chakra 1-5

Chronic Fatigue—Any and All Chakras

Circulation Problems—Chakra 1-5

Cirrhosis—Any and All Chakras

Colds and Influenza—Chakra 1, 4

Colitis—Chakra 1, 2, 3, and 4

Common Cold—Chakra 4, 5, 6, and 7

Congestion—Chakra 4, 5, 6, and 7

Constipation—Chakra 1, 2, and 3

Cough—Chakra 4, 5, and 6

Cramps—Chakra 1, 2, and 3

Crohn's Disease—Chakra 1, 2, and 3

Cysts—Chakra 1, 2, 3, and 4

Depression—Chakra 2, 3, 4, and 5

Diabetes—Chakra 2, 3, and 4

Diarrhea—Chakra 1, 2, and 3

Dizziness—Chakra 4, 5, 6, and 7

Ear Problems—Chakra 4, 5, and 6

Eczema—Chakra 1, 2, 3, and 4

Edema—Chakra 2, 3, and 4

Elbow Problems—Chakra 2, 3, and 4

Emphysema—Chakra 1, 2, 3, and 4

Endometriosis—Chakra 1, 2, 3, and 4

Epilepsy—Chakra 4, 5, and 6

Eye Problems—Chakra 1, 2, 3, 4, 5, and 6

Fainting—All the Chakras

Fatigue—Chakra 1, 2, 3, and 4

Feet Problems—Chakra 1, 2, and 3

Fever—Chakra 1, 2, 3, and 4

Fibroid Tumors & Cysts—Chakra 1-4

Flu—Chakra 4, 5, 6, and 7

Fluid Retention—Any and All Chakra

Gallstones—Chakra 3, 4

Gas Pains (Flatulence)—Chakra 1-4, and 6

Goiter—Chakra 4, 5, and 6

Gout—Chakra 1, 2, 3, and 4

Grave's Disease—Any and All Chakras

Hair Loss—Chakra 2, 3, 6, and 7

Hay Fever—Chakra 1, 4, and 6

Headaches—Chakra 3, 5, and 6

Hearing Problems—Chakra 5 and 6

Heartburn—Chakra 3, 4

Heart Problems—Chakra 1, 2, 3, and 4

Hemorrhoids—Chakra 1, 2, and 3

Hepatitis—Any and All Chakras

Herpes—Chakra 2, 3, and 4

High Blood Pressure—Any and All Chakras

Hyperglycemia—Chakra 1, 3

Hypoglycemia—Chakra 1, 3

Immune Problems—Any and All Chakras

Impotence—Chakra 1, 2, and 4

Incontinence—Chakra 1, 2, and 3

Indigestion—Chakra 3, 4

Infection—Chakra 3, 4, and 5

Infertility—Chakra 1, 2, 3, and 4

Inflammation—Chakra 1, 3, and 4

Insomnia—Chakra 1, 6, and 7

Irritable Bowel Syndrome—Chakra 1- 4

Jar Problems—Chakra 1, 3, 4, and 5

Jaundice—Any and All Chakras

Joint Problems—Chakra 2, 3, and 4

Kidney Problems—Chakra 3, 4, and 5

Kidney Stones—Chakra 1, 4, and 5

Knee Problems—Chakra 1, 2, 3, 4, and 5

Lactose Intolerance—Chakra 1, 2, and 3

Laryngitis—Chakra 3, 4, and 5

Leg Problems—Chakra 1, 2

Leukemia—Chakra 1, 3, and 6

Liver Problems—Chakra 1, 3, 4, and 5

Lou Gehrig's disease—Any and All Chakras

Lumps—Any and All Chakras

Lung Problems—Chakra 3, 4

Lupus—Chakra 1, 3, and 5

Lymph Problems—Chakra 4, 6, and 7

Lymphoma—Any and All Chakras

Measles—Any and All Chakras

Menopausal Problems—Chakra 1, 2, and 4

Menstrual Problems—Chakra 1, 2, and 3

Migraines—Chakra 2, 4, and 6

Mononucleosis—Chakra 4, 5, 6, and 7

Motion Sickness—Chakra 3, 5, 6, and 7

Multiple Sclerosis (MS)—Chakra 1, 4

Muscular Dystrophy—Chakra 2, 4, and 6

Nail Biting—Chakra 1, 3, and 6

Nausea—Chakra 2, 3

Neck Problems—Chakra 1, 5, and 6

Neuralgia—Chakra 3, 5

Nose Problems—Chakra 4, 5, and 6

Numbness—All the Chakras

Obesity—Chakra 1, 2, 3, and 4

Osteoporosis—Chakra 1, 2, 3, and 4

Ovarian Cancer—Chakra 1, 2, 3, and 4

Pain—Chakra 3, 4

Pancreatic Problems—Chakra 2, 3, and 4

Panic Attack—Chakra 3, 4, 5, 6 and 7

Parkinson's—Any and All Chakras

Psoriasis—Chakra 1, 2, and 3

Respiratory Ailments—Chakra 2, 3, and 4

Rheumatism—Chakra 3, 4

Sciatica—Chakra 1, 2

Seasickness—Chakra 1, 2

Seizures—Chakra 2, 3, 4, 5, and 6

Shingles—Chakra 3, 4, and 5

Shoulder Problems—Chakra 4, 5, and 6

Skin Problems—Chakra 1, 2, and 3

Snoring—Chakra 3, 4, and 5

Spleen Problem—Chakra 1, 2, 3, 4, and 5

Stomach Problems—Chakra 2, 3

Stroke—Chakra 1, 3, 4, and 6

Swelling—Chakra 5, 6

Syphilis—Chakra 2, 3, and 4

Teeth Problems—Chakra 1, 2, 3, 4, 5, and 6

Thymus—Chakra 1, 2, 4, and 5

Thyroid—Chakra 1, 5

Tumors—Chakra 3, 4

Ulcers—Chakra 1, 3, 4

Varicose Veins—Chakra 1, 4

Venereal Disease—Chakra 1, 2, 3, and 4

Yeast Infections—Chakra 2, 3, and 4

About the Author

Francine Milford, BS, LMT, CTN, is a state and nationally licensed massage therapist, personal trainer and Holistic Practitioner. She is the owner and creator of the Reiki Center of Venice. She is an inspirational teacher and continuing education provider for many National Certifying Boards.

Francine Milford has attained Reiki Mastership through several lineages and brings her combined knowledge of energy work into her classes. Having experience in the Fitness Industry as a Personal Trainer and Aerobics Instructor, she has created a series of workshops and classes that combine the Body, the Mind, and the Spirit.

"I teach courses in Tuning Fork Therapy® and offer eight levels of training manuals. I believe in empowering my students."

www.ReikiCenterofVenice.com

www.TuningForkTherapy.com

www.FrancineMilford.com

www.KomyoReiki.com

www.SoundsGoodtoMePublishing.com

www.ingramcontent.com/pod-product-compliance
Lightning Source LLC
Chambersburg PA
CBHW081259170426
43198CB00017B/2845